Journal

365+ writing prompts, ideas and quotes to
cultivate joy and well-being

Journal

365+ writing prompts, ideas and
quotes to cultivate joy
and well-being

Judy Shafarman

New Vision

Publications

10 9 8 7 6 5 4 3 2

Printed in the United States of America; simultaneously
published in the United Kingdom, European Union,
India and Australia

ISBN: 978-1494458966

www.Judyshafarman.net

*Blessings and love to many a student
and teacher over many a year and especially to
Janis W. Shafarman, a.k.a., Mom*

Introduction

> *Writing is a form of therapy; sometimes I wonder how all those who do not write, compose, or paint can manage to escape the madness, melancholia, the panic and fear which is inherent in a human situation.*

So wrote Graham Greene in his 1980 book, *Ways of Escape.* Keeping a journal is not about writing an extraordinary memoir nor meant for anyone else to see; you can do that too, but journal writing is essentially private.

A journal can be a confidante, a cheerleader, or an anthropology professor who trains you in objective observation skills. Inside its pages you can build and equip your special closet in which secrets can be hidden, skeletons buried, and castle designs drafted. The journal is the place where feelings and ideas are not discounted; ranting, crying, bragging and exulting cannot be judged as inappropriate.

Oh if you want to get all digital and 21st century, it is okay to tap on some sort of computer keyboard. I'm more of a 20th century kind of person. I love to use my comfortable favorite pen and bound notebook and I find handwriting to be more intimate than keyboarding. Understandably, though, many other people prefer the security of password protection and the fact that computer files are so easily preserved and transferable to other locations, not to mention revisable if a great poem, song or other inspiration pours forth. There's also a soothing quality to the regular clicking of key tapping.

I kept journals even back in the day when they were called diaries in junior high school. Later when I was in college, I tried my hand at poetry and sometimes dreamed of being a fiction writer. I also wrote wails and whines that *they* don't understand me; well, *they* was mostly my hard-working single mom whose voice will live forever in some corner of my mind

Before starting out, I have a confession; I have never yet managed to write every single day for a full uninterrupted period of 12 months in a row. So, go ahead make your writing an imperfect practice or even a cherished ritual, just not a dreaded obligation to cross off of a "to do" list. Remember the goal is to feel happier than before, not more burdened.

I typically carry a small, portable notebook for when I'll be in waiting rooms or on public transportation or even hit with an idea near a park bench. My journals are only 40 pages long and quite nondescript. I have dozens of completed simple notebooks with all sorts of covers in a box somewhere with a note attached to destroy upon my death. Actually since I almost never look at them, I could get rid of them myself, but I am a bit of the sentimental hoarding type. I have at times had a good rip up of anger-filled pages.

My preference for the simplest of notebooks derives from not wanting to be put off by what to write on that first virgin white page that would be in a fancy bound book along with the freedom to destroy pages that no longer hold utility in my memory. (Spiral notebooks are great for removing pages destined to be burned or shredded.)

If you don't wish to use a small notebook or a computer file, an even more casual, unintimidating suggestion is to write on legal pad style paper in white or your favorite pastel color. You can store the filled pages in plain envelopes, ringed binders or simply discard them periodically. You can even scrawl on any sort of remnant paper such as the back side of printouts if you're not writing for your grandchildren or one-day biographer.

The utility of organizing and putting thoughts down is the point of the process, not the posterity of such mind wanderings. The act of writing becomes an agent of change even when you don't make resolutions about action steps and deadlines.

Keeping an introspective journal or record serves various purposes. One is to reflect on, and set in words, gratitude for each day and blessings in having a functioning body, roof, food and all the loving people and possessions you wish to bless (your body home and food may not be perfect, but they keep you going and you can be thankful for them no matter what). Keeping a gratitude journal is a powerful mood-elevating tool universally recommended in the positive psychology movement. Along with the upbeat accounts of what happens in your days, you will find your own clues into how to be a better, happier individual (so is the goal).

Another key objective in keeping a journal is to do a free flow of whatever is on your mind. Some business folks call this "taking a brain dump," "doing a mind sweep," "mind scanning," or "a brain drain." These inelegant terms reflect the process of putting down in words whatever it is that flits into your thoughts before going to sleep at night or while taking showers or walks. So, the words which pour out can be anything from storming anger, dreams for launching the most fabulous enterprise and reaping millions of dollars and wild accolades, to impassioned complaints about "why can't *they* do things the way that they *should*"?

Julia Cameron teaches people to develop their artistic and imaginative selves in her transformative book, *The Artist's Way*, first published in 1992. She insists on daily, free association writing to unblock creativity and instructs her students to undertake an exercise called "morning pages." I started writing morning pages more than 10 years ago when I followed the Artist's Way course with a small group of women while making stressful transitions in my life (including divorce and moving). I've been a fan of Julia Cameron ever since and like her, prefer my own writing voice early in the morning rather than later in the day or before going to sleep at night.

Cameron's recommendation is to sit alone with pen and paper shortly after waking up and freely hand write without stopping to reflect for 3 full-size pages. Among other results, this sort of writing serves to heal and eliminate from our minds petty annoyances of one-time negative interactions and recurring *junk*. Free-association writing of this type may provide both artists and business leaders with fresh thinking and even great creative surges. Consequently, fans of brain draining rave about it.

Try getting up in the morning, doing whatever you need to do to wake up and get everyone else (children or spouse) on his or her path, and then take your journal back to bed or to your favorite space and curl up for a nice 15-30 minute respite. Or even better, RPJ: rise, pee, journal, if possible, and record your dreams and first thoughts with no stopping to edit. In my experience, the more regular and consistent my writing routine, the more likely I am to sift out gold nuggets from the regular dirt. Writing is an endurance exercise that I hope to continue on most days as long as I'm alive.

I have another word or three about the mechanics of keeping a journal. I always date my journal entries and even put in a time because sometimes I'll write a few times in the course of a day on a burning topic and I like to follow my progression of mood and thought. Another journal keeper I know writes a one or two word weather bulletin at the top of all of his entries (i.e., sunny, gloomy gray, or rainy) to see if the free flow writing correlates with the weather. You may choose to start each entry with a mood or health bulletin. Examples of a journal entry might begin: Thursday, Feb. 9, 8:30 am, gray, rainy and I'm really feeling blah today. Or, Friday, Oct. 16, 7:35 am, woke up stiff but happy.

Keeping a journal for the purpose of scanning our minds facilitates the processing of what happened in the past as well as a clarification of our thinking. It provides an outlet for making sense of the world around us, our feelings, and desires in our hearts. A journal is a place to make records, outline memories, conversations and current events for later processing and decoding.

The journal is where I can write about so-called "growth opportunities" from my daily encounters so that maybe such agonies don't have to be re-enacted (as Barbra Streisand sings, "there are no mistakes, only lessons to be learned.") The journal is also the place to ask questions without knowing the answers, undertake thought experiments, and dream gorgeous colorful visions for the future.

Today in the world of social media, millions of people choose to share their writings including income reports, parenting challenges, and personal foibles on blogs and in 140 character twitter feeds. That may be your preference. Alternatively, you might decide to have one special buddy or a very small coffee klatch with whom to share your journal entries; either of these more intimate choices sounds more meaningful to my private 20th century sensibilities. Make sure your personal choices elevate you and your sense of self; you

9

don't want to feel criticized or as if you have to write a final edited copy with all the i's dotted, problems resolved, and plotlines finished.

My primary intention in creating this book is to encourage solitary introspective journaling as a cultivator for gratitude, appreciation, reflection, and ultimately, joy. The prompts and quotes included in this book may at first look evoke some repetition, but each time you read and write, you will see, think and write with new "eyes" and new thinking. The second or third time you write on the same subject and emotions might well be a huge revelatory breakthrough journal entry.

As you're settling into your writing routine, consider other motives for writing beyond the format of this book. Personal computer files, notebooks, or journals are good for such uses as:

1. monitoring food intake, exercise, and healthy behaviors (or unhealthy, as the case may be)
2. monitoring medical conditions or symptoms
3. keeping records of financial outlays and income
4. preserving memories, perhaps in a scrapbook style with photos and memorabilia
5. using words to paint the scenes and store the memories of your trips, i.e., a travel diary
6. sparking creativity, e.g., ideas for art projects or home décor

7. keeping to-do lists and recording goals attained
8. weighing pros and cons before making a decision
9. clarifying values, priorities and perspectives.
10. giving yourself a locker room, pre-game pep talk,
    confidence booster before a big meeting or presentation
11. taking notes at a lecture, in a class or whenever, wherever and however new information is being acquired in order to reinforce your memory
12. writing "letters" to your children or other loved ones and perhaps even writing their "replies" in order to understand differences in outlook (try using your non-dominant hand for the reply letter)
13. composing letters from your 100 year old self to your present self or from your present self to the person you were when you were 18 (as therapeutic reflection)
14. expounding on ideas for solving the ills of the world
15. writing down jokes
16. rehearsing in a script or role play for painful conversations
17. drafting ideas for application essays or difficult letters that need to be written

18. recording the health and behaviors of plants in your garden
19. recording the health and behavior of children in your family
20. congratulating yourself on your successes and delving into ways to do the job even better next time
21. keeping a chronology of your life as a straightforward non-reflective diary
22. recounting dreams upon waking for later interpretation
23. keeping a record of recipes, menus, and how you entertained
24. documenting observations that can be useful in social or professional situations
25. setting down quotations you like
26. playing with language, writing limericks, haiku, songs, or other general poetry
27. starting or developing short stories, novels, or plays
28. Writing about the great exploits of your life for your descendants or the world at large, i.e., your autobiography or memoirs

Journaling is my platform to say whatever I want but especially to process my feelings, make sense of the world, and give expression to gratitude and daily pleasures. No matter what it is that's irking me and trying to get out of me and onto paper, I can always come back to a blessing that, for example, I don't live in a teeming reeking ghetto, sick with malaria in a house made of cardboard and no knowledge of where I'll get tomorrow's food. Writing lets me luxuriate in being literate in English which I've loved endlessly since my first Roald Dahl and Judy Blume nights with a flashlight in bed after "lights out" when I was in elementary school.

Each day in the year or twenty that you use this book, I've given you a quotation to promote joy and well-being along with an idea either for writing or reflection. For those of you who want to strengthen your creativity muscles, I've also included 25 more imaginative journal prompts for when the muse shows up in addition to a few other whimsical prompts here and there. At the end of the book, you'll also find two appendices with a few more writers' words on writing and folk wisdom which you can also journal about.

Whenever this book comes into your hands, start to write. Don't worry about skipping days or holding off until January; this is not a test of your fortitude. If your writing routine has been dormant or non-existent, I assure you that your sense of well-being will increase through the time you regularly take in solitude to unload what's nagging at you and express gratitude for the good things in your life.

(A small aside for those who learned multiple languages in childhood or have other challenges which might make writing a true chore or clash with the spell checker: there are no points off for spelling or other mistakes, but you don't actually have to write. You can of course simply reflect or use a voice recorder.)

Go on, open up your private facebook page or twitter feed with no need for anyone's approval or comments. Start your own log, not blog. Cultivate joy and a better life with the words you write and utter.

Postscript for the printed book: I was going to draw in the margins and add some of my own pizzazz before publication, but I opted to suggest that you do your own doodles with colors and styles of your choosing just as you might in your actual journal.

Be free not just with colors but also with mind maps, outlined points, circles, arrows, columns, sketches and so on and on and on.

January 1

Twenty years from now you will be more disappointed by the things that you didn't do than by the ones you did do.

Mark Twain

Writing: A dream of mine is to . . .

January 2

The ideal day never comes. Today is ideal for him who makes it so.
Horatio Dresser

Writing: An ideal day for me in January would include:

January 3

Great opportunities to help others seldom come, but small ones surround us every day.
Sally Koch

Writing: I felt so good when I helped . . .
to . . .   or:
When . . . helped me, I felt . . .

January 4

How old would you be if you didn't know how old you are?

Age is a case of mind over matter. If you don't mind, it don't matter.

Both quotes are from Satchel Paige who was the oldest rookie in Major League Baseball at the age of 42 (in 1948, after being a phenomenon in the Negro Baseball leagues for some 22 years)

Writing: What do I think of my present age? How old would I like to be?

January 5

Like all great travelers, I remember more
than I have seen and I have seen more than
I remember.
Benjamin Disraeli

Writing: [This quote was seen painted in
huge white letters on a black brick wall on
the side of a hotel in Amsterdam in the
summer of 2013]. What travels would I like
to write about and what distorted memory
of traveling?

January 6

Life is uncharted territory. It reveals its story
one moment at a time.
Leo Buscaglia

Writing: A story revealed to me is /was
. . .   What is the story that debilitates me
and what story elevates me?

January 7

Every child is an artist. The problem is how to remain an artist once he grows up.
Pablo Picasso

Writing: I love the way I let my child self out when I . . .

January 8

Who seeks more than he has, hinders himself from enjoying what he has.
Solomon Ibn Gibriol

Writing: I am very appreciative that I have so much . . .

January 9

Perhaps too much of everything is as bad as too little.
Edna Ferber

Writing: What abundance there is in my life, but also a bit too much of . . .

January 10

I don't believe that life is supposed to make you feel good, or to make you feel miserable either. Life is just supposed to make you feel.
Gloria Naylor

Writing: Thinking about . . . I feel . . .

January 11

If there were in the world today any large
number of people who desired their own
happiness more than they desired the
unhappiness of others, we could have a
paradise in a few years.
Bertrand Russell

Writing: Oh yes I have known that feeling
expressed in the German word,
schadenfreude, which translates to "damage-
joy" when we gloat over someone else's
pain. I felt it when . . .

January 12

Never fear shadows. They simply mean
there's a light shining somewhere nearby.
Ruth E. Renkel

Writing: Okay, let's do an interview. Self,
what's your deepest fear? What would you
do if you knew you couldn't fail? How
would you live if you won the lottery and
didn't need to earn a living for the rest of
your life? Why aren't you living closer to
that reality right now?

January 13

If you are happy and people around you are
not happy, they will not allow you to stay
happy. Therefore much of our happiness
depends upon our ability to spread
happiness around us.
Dr. Madan Kataria

Writing: Well yes, I can spread happiness,
but I can also see beyond the complainers
and pessimists? When and why do I
complain or feel pessimistic?

January 14

Those who dwell among the beauties and
mysteries of the Earth are never alone or
weary of life.
Rachel Carson

Writing: I have always wondered about . . .

January 15

We must learn to live together as brothers
or we will perish together as fools.
 Martin Luther King, Jr.

Writing: What a world of diverse world of
people of all ages and cultures around me.
Today I can appreciate . . .

January 16

Darkness cannot drive out darkness;
only light can do that. Hate cannot drive out
hate; only love can do that.
Martin Luther King Jr.

Writing: I'm shining light on . . .

January 17

Be willing to have it so.
William James

Writing: What was so hard for me that I
can accept today?

January 18

Think for yourself and let others enjoy the
privilege of doing so too.
 Voltaire

Writing: I love about myself my own
unique   way of . . .

January 19

A happy person is not a person in a certain set of circumstances, but rather a person with a certain set of attitudes. When you try to understand everything, you will not understand anything. The best way is to understand yourself, and then you will understand everything.
Shunryu Suzuki

Writing: Just for now, I can focus on myself and my particular strengths and weaknesses.

January 20

Persons thankful for the little things are
certain to be the ones with much to be
thankful for.
Frank Clark

Writing: Yippee! I am so thankful for . . .

January 21

A weed is no more than a flower in disguise.
James Lowell

Writing: Whether I envision a daffodil or a
rose, I will appreciate its own specific beauty
and aroma. Even a dandelion can be seen
as beautiful.   What odd beauty do I find in
something or someone that's not classically
formed?

January 22

Laughter is a form of internal jogging. It moves your internal organs around. It enhances respiration. It is an igniter of great expectations.
Norman Cousins

Writing: What do I think about Cousin's contention that "laughter is the best medicine"? How do I feel about conventional and alternative health care medicine? What can the power of the mind do to heal the pains of the body?

January 23

Pessimism leads to weakness, optimism to power.
William James.

Writing: I have so much strength and power today.

January 24

If a person's basic state of mind is serene
and calm, then it is possible for this inner
peace to overwhelm a painful physical
experience. On the other hand, if
someone is suffering from depression,
anxiety, or any form of emotional distress,
then even if he or she happens to be
enjoying physical comforts, he will not really
be able to experience the happiness that
these could bring.
The Dalai Lama

Writing: What suffering and distress have I
felt recently? What might bring me some
tranquility?

January 25

The meaning of things lies not in the things themselves, but in our attitude towards them.
Antoine de Saint-Exupery

Writing and task: Hello feelings. How are you today? Before writing today, I can take a look in the best mirror I have and talk to myself. Now, I smile, blow a kiss to the glass and go and write.

January 26

Life is not a matter of milestones, but of moments.
Rose Kennedy

Writing: Yesterday or today, I had a spectacular moment when . . .

January 27

Think it more satisfactory to live richly
than to die rich.
Sir Thomas Browne

Writing: I am dreaming of indulging in . .
.

January 28

I think the one lesson I have learned is that
there is no substitute for paying attention.
 Diane Sawyer

Writing: I'm going to focus my attention on
. . .

January 29

From what we get, we can make a living;
what we give, however, makes a life.
Arthur Ashe

Writing: My life is full of . . .

January 30

Kindness is more important than wisdom,
and the recognition of this is the beginning
of wisdom.
Theodore Isaac Rubin

Writing: When I . . . , I felt . . .

January 31

Don't ask yourself what the world needs;
ask yourself what makes you come alive and
then go and do that because what the world
needs is people who have come alive.
Harold Whitman

Writing: Whoopee! My life is full of . . .

February 1

Have faith in your dreams and someday
your rainbow will come smiling through.
No matter how your heart is grieving if you
keep on believing, the dream that you wish
will come true.
from Cinderella

Writing: My life as fairytale:

February 2

The first recipe for happiness is: avoid too
lengthy meditation on the past.
André Maurois

Writing: Today I am thrilled by . . .

February 3

We meet ourselves time and again in a
thousand disguises on the path of life.
Carl Jung

Writing: That mask I wear,   "the stranger
inside myself":

February 4

Only those who will risk going too far can
possibly find out how far they can go.
T. S Elliot

Writing: What risk will I take in the next 24
hours?

February 5

Just as a cautious businessman avoids
investing all his capital in one concern, so
wisdom would probably admonish us also
not to anticipate all our happiness from one
quarter alone.
Sigmund Freud

Writing: Lately I've been neglecting . . .
maybe now is the time to do something
about that.

February 6

Time is the coin of your life. It is the only
coin you have, and only you can determine
how it will be spent. Be careful lest you let
other people spend it for you.
Carl Sandburg

Writing: My time is valuable. I can re-
allocate it or cherish it by nurturing my well-
being every day.

February 7

This is my "depressed stance." When you're depressed, it makes a lot of difference how you stand. The worst thing you can do is straighten up and hold your head high because then you'll start to feel better. If you're going to get any joy out of being depressed, you've got to stand like this.
Charlie Brown, a.k.a., Charles M. Schulz creator of *Peanuts*

Writing: Sit up and take notice! How's my posture and body language working for me? Have I been putting on the confidence stance lately?

February 8

Finish each day and be done with it. You
have done what you could; some blunders
and absurdities have crept in; forget them as
soon as you can. Tomorrow is a new day;
you shall begin it serenely and with too high
a spirit to be encumbered with your old
nonsense.
Ralph Waldo Emerson

Writing: In the castle of my mind, I feel
agitated or dis-eased when my mind
wanders into the closet of . . . but I feel
serene when I dance into the ballroom of . .

February 9

We are all teachers and students to each
other, and we are never finished in either
role.
Lee L. Jampolsky

Writing: Who and what can I teach this
week?

February 10

It is not what we see and touch or that
which others do for us which makes us
happy; it is that which we think and feel and
do, first for the other fellow and then for
ourselves.
Helen Keller

Writing: I value . . .

February 11

Your future has nothing to do with getting
somewhere you think you need to be.
It has to do with the awareness that getting
there means being here.
Carl A. Hammerschlag

Writing: Book title from John Kabat-Zinn
on mindfulness: Wherever you go, there you
are. I'm with me all the time; I might as well
love myself now. Let's start with . . .

February 12

I have noticed that folks are generally about
as happy as they make up their minds to be.
Abraham Lincoln

Writing: How busy has my mind been
lately? How busy do I want it to be?

February 13

A loving person lives in a loving world. A
hostile person lives in a hostile world:
everyone you meet is your mirror.
Ken Keyes Jr.

Writing: Oh, nuts, that irritating behavior in
my near and dear one, might it be my own
character shortcoming?

February 14

The greatest good you can do for another is
not just to share your riches, but to reveal to
him his own.
Benjamin Disraeli

Writing: I will write an appreciation to . . .
and even share some or all of my words
with this important person in my life.

February 15

The more I travelled the more I realized
that fear makes strangers of people that
should be friends.
Shirley MacLaine

Writing: When it comes to . . . I can
pretend to be fearless today.

February 16

During your life, everything you do and
everyone you meet rubs off in some way.
Some bit of everything you experience stays
with everyone you've ever known, and
nothing is lost. That's what's eternal, these
little specks of experience in a great,
enormous river that has no end.
Harriet Doerr

Writing: What unexpected experiences
rubbed off on me to make me into who I
am today?

February 17

A man is happy so long as he chooses to be
happy and nothing can stop him.
Alexander Solzenitsyn

Writing: I choose . . .

February 18

Life is not the way it's supposed to be. It's
the way it is. The way you cope with it is
what makes the difference.
Virginia Satir

Writing: Synonyms for cope: manage,
handle, deal with. What's on my mind now?
With what am I now coping and how am I
doing with that?

February 19

True responsibility is to allow yourself to
see higher inner worlds that you now resist
seeing. The limit of your view of the
universe is not the limit of the universe.
Self-newness is revelation, not creation. So
make inner progress. Real progress is when
you learn something you thought you
already knew.
Vernon Howard

Writing: Now I see exactly what I already
knew about . . .

February 20

We are the sculptors of our day. We can
mold it creatively into a wonderful
masterpiece. We control the amount of
moisture we mix into our clay. We pound
it, shape it, stroke it, love it. Others can
offer suggestions, and we gain new
perspectives from their advice, but it is
finally our own creation. Our knife may
occasionally slip, or our mixture of earth
may be too dry. Any great artist suffers
temporary setbacks. Besides, imperfections
in art often make it all the more interesting.
Source unknown

Writing: If I had uncountable hours, space
and money, what creative workspace would
I design and what creative work would I
undertake therein?

February 21

Far away there in the sunshine are my
highest aspirations. I may not reach them,
but I can look up and see their beauty,
believe in them and try to follow where they
lead.
Louisa May Alcott

Writing: What pot of gold would I love to
find at the end of a rainbow?

February 22

The foolish man seeks happiness in the
distance;
the wise grows it under his feet.
James Oppenheim

Writing: Hey, I can be happy with what is.
I don't have to look to what I want to get.
I am so happy that . . .

February 23

You are a child of the Universe, no less than the moon and the stars; you have a right to be here. And whether or not it is clear to you, no doubt the Universe is unfolding as it should.
Max Ehrmann

Writing: What "unfolding" of the universe is taking more time than I wish it would? Am I doing my part to achieve my desired ends?

Ehrmann wrote "Desiderata" in 1927 as a sort of prayer. This prose-poem, now in the public domain, became extremely popular on posters and greeting cards in the 1970s and 80s (to the point of corniness and parodies). Go on, read it aloud in your silly or super somber voice.

Desiderata

Go placidly amid the noise and haste, and remember what peace there may be in silence. As far as possible without surrender, be on good terms with all persons. Speak your truth quietly and clearly; and listen to others, even the dull and the ignorant; they too have their story. Avoid loud and aggressive persons, they are vexations to the spirit. If you compare yourself with others, you may become vain and bitter; for always there will be greater and lesser persons than yourself. Enjoy your achievements as well as your plans. Keep interested in your own career, however humble; it is a real possession in the changing fortunes of time. Exercise caution in your business affairs for the world is full of trickery. But let this not blind you to what virtue there is; many persons strive for high ideals; and everywhere life is full of heroism. Be yourself. Especially, do not feign affection. Neither be cynical about love; for in the face of all aridity and disenchantment it is as perennial as the grass. Take kindly the counsel of the years, gracefully surrendering the things of youth. Nurture strength of spirit to shield you in sudden misfortune. But do not distress yourself with dark imaginings. Many fears are born of fatigue and loneliness. Beyond a wholesome discipline, be gentle with yourself. You are a child of the universe, no less than the trees and the stars; you have a right to be here. And whether or not it is clear to you, no doubt the universe is unfolding as it should. Therefore be at peace with God, whatever you conceive Him to be, and whatever your labors and aspirations, in the noisy confusion of life keep peace with your soul. With all its sham, drudgery, and broken dreams, it is still a beautiful world. Be cheerful. Strive to be happy.

February 24

So long as we love we serve;
So long as we are loved by others,
I would almost say that we are
indispensable;
And no one is useless while they have a
friend.
Robert Louis Stevenson

Writing: I'm a bit annoyed now because of
what was said by. . . .
At the same time, I so appreciate . . .

February 25

The fountain of content must spring up in
the mind, and he who has so little
knowledge of human nature as to seek
happiness by changing anything but his own
disposition will waste his life in fruitless
efforts and multiply the grief which he
purposes to remove.
 Samuel Johnson

Writing: How is my disposition on this fine
day? Does it fluctuate when the sky is gray
or sunny? What observation will give me a
smile as I write?

February 26

The great opportunity is where you are. Do not despise your own place and hour. Every place is under the stars, every place is the center of the world.
John Burroughs

Writing: Who and what is in the center of my world?

February 27

It has long been an axiom of mine that the little things are infinitely more important.
Sir Arthur Conan Doyle

Writing: I am so grateful for all of these little things in my life:

February 28

A knowledge of the path cannot be
substituted for putting one foot in front of
the other.
M. C. Richards

Writing: Oh, I have to *take action*. Well,
what teeny tiny action steps can I set down
in a list for me to do in the merry month of
March?

February 29

I will love the light for it shows me the way,
yet I will endure the darkness for it shows
me the stars.
Og Mandino

Writing: What darkness is still holed up in
my soul and how can I shine some light on
it?

March 1

One bulb at a time. There was no other way
to do it. No shortcuts--simply loving the
slow process of planting. Loving the work
as it unfolded, loving an achievement that
grew slowly and bloomed for only three
weeks each year.
Jaroldeen Asplund Edward

Writing: What can I plant this season and
have the patience to let it grow in its own
time?

March 2

We have to dare to be ourselves however
frightening or strange that self may prove to
be.
May Sarton

Writing: I am exploring who I am today
without masks and artifice.

March 3

If we can just let go and trust that things will work out the way they're supposed to, without trying to control the outcome, then we can begin to enjoy the moment more fully. The joy of the freedom it brings becomes more pleasurable than the experience itself.
Goldie Hawn

Writing: In this moment I feel . . .
Doing this writing gives me time to reflect on . . .

March 4

The first principle is that you must not fool
yourself-and you are the easiest person to
fool.
Richard Feynman

Writing: Oh well, I can get down on myself
today for that foolish thing I did or said, or
I can celebrate my imperfect humanity.
Hooray for my beautiful imperfections! I
am proud that . . .

March 5

The gathering of facts does not make for
the understanding of life. Knowing is one
thing, and understanding another.
Knowledge does not lead to understanding;
but understanding may enrich knowledge,
and knowledge may implement
understanding.
Jiddu Krishnamurti

Writing: Ten years ago, I didn't grasp it, but
now I understand. . .

March 6

The nature of rain is the same, but it makes
thorns grow in the marshes and flowers in
the garden.
Unknown

Writing: Blessed rain. Beautiful flowers.
Nature's poetry.

March 7

Learn to get in touch with the silence within
yourself, and know that everything in life
has purpose. There are no mistakes, no
coincidences, all events are blessings given
to us to learn from.
Elisabeth Kubler-Ross

Writing: Now I will breathe and enjoy a
moment of silence and then free write.

March 8

Those who flow through life as life flows,
feel no wear, feel no tear, need no mending,
no repair.
Lao Tzu

Writing: I'm still sitting with some pain and
anger about . . . How can I get into life
flow today?

March 9

Worry is a thin stream of fear trickling
through the mind. If you don't take action,
it cuts a channel into which all other
thoughts are drained.
Arthur Somers Roche

Writing: Woo hoo, yippee, hooray, I'm
going to love myself and give myself the
following gifts of time, attention, and
sensual pleasure:

March 10

When I dare to be powerful — to use my strength in the service of my vision, then it becomes less and less important whether I am afraid.
Audre Lorde

Writing: Fritz Perls wrote that, "fear is excitement without the breath."   What does that mean to me? What deep breath excitement can I feel in my gut? I am powerful enough and fearless enough today to . . .

March 11

If you cry because the sun has gone out of your life, your tears will prevent you from seeing the stars.
Rabindranath Tagore

Writing: The last time I indulged in a cathartic crying jag was . . . What triggered that crying spell? Would it help me now to cry about the pains I've felt? What stars would I see after wiping away the tears?

March 12

And the day came when the risk it took to remain tight in a bud was more painful than the risk it took to blossom.
 Anaïs Nin

Writing: When I . . . , I can blossom. When specifically and how can I flourish more in what I love?

March 13

If you take a flower in your hand and really look at it, it's your world for the moment.
 Georgia O' Keefe

Writing: How is living in the past or future thinking serving me or hindering me in my life? How much time do I want to devote to daydreaming about the future? How does daydreaming and future planning impact on my enjoyment of the present?

March 14

This is the last of human freedoms-- to choose one's attitude in any given set of circumstances, to choose one's own way.
 Victor Frankl

Writing: No matter what, I can always adjust my attitude. How am I feeling today?

March 15

Even if you are on the right track you will
get run over if you just sit there.
Will Rogers

Writing: Man, oh man, I do all this writing
to be happier, and I'm still stuck with
occasional ruminations about . . . Today I
can write it out and let it fly away.

Person who annoys me, I send you forth on
your own life course and path of personal
growth. I am moving on.

March 16

The true measure of a man is how he treats
someone who can do him absolutely no
good.
Ann Landers

Writing: The value of politeness and good
manners in the world is called *derech eretz* in
Hebrew, the way in the world. How can I
cultivate being nice(r) this week, and my
way of being in my community?

March 17

Every now and then take a good look at
something not made with hands -- a
mountain, a star, the turn of a stream. There
will come to you wisdom, and patience, and
solace, and above all the assurance that you
are not alone in the world.
Sidney Lovet

Writing: How utterly absolutely wonderful
that my solitude is my choosing and I am
never really alone in the world. Who would
be a joy to contact?

March 18

The world of reality has limits. The world of
imagination is boundless.
Jean Jacques Rousseau

Writing: Think of Dr. Seuss (Theodor
Geisel) who went where no children's book
author had been before with imagined
animals, fantastic pictures and made-up
words all in rhyme. I can see the world in
new colors, smells and sounds while I write
in my journal today.

March 19

I was neurotic for years. I was anxious and depressed and selfish. Everyone kept telling me to change. I resented them, and I agreed with them, and I wanted to change, but simply couldn't, no matter how hard I tried. Then one day someone said to me, "Don't change. I love you just as you are." Those words were music to my ears: "Don't change. Don't change. Don't change- I love you as you are." I relaxed. I came alive. And suddenly I changed!
Anthony de Mello

Writing: I can simply love myself just the way I am.   I love the way I . . .

March 20

Those who can laugh without cause have
either found the true meaning of happiness
or have gone stark raving mad.
Norm Papernick

Writing: Equinox madness. Celebrate
the change of seasons. I am in love with

March 21

Since you get more joy out of giving joy to
others, you should put a good deal more
thought into the happiness that you are able
to give.
Eleanor Roosevelt

Writing: I feel so good about the "good
deed" I did when I . . .

March 22

Our main business is not to see what lies
dimly at a distance but to do what lies
clearly at hand.
Thomas Carlysle

(This quote comes from one of the
forebears of self development books, people
influencer Dale Carnegie's *How to Stop
Worrying and Start Living* first published in
1948 when Carnegie was past 60.)

Writing: What will I do today/tomorrow?

March 23

I've grown to realize the joy that comes
from little victories is preferable to the fun
that comes from ease and the pursuit of
pleasure.
Lawana Blackwell

Writing: I will put effort into . . . and
gain earned satisfaction from . . . within
this proposed timeline of tiny turtle steps or
snail slides:

March 24

Every exit is an entry somewhere else.
Tom Stoppard

Writing: I'm an actor on the stage in my
mind. I will write or draw my stage and set
and consider my place upon it.

March 25

I need to take an emotional breath, step
back and remind myself who's actually in
charge of my life.
Judith Knowlton

Writing: Today's writing is a deep breath
and meditation about . . .

March 26

The time you enjoy wasting is
not wasted time.
Bertrand Russell

Writing: To me this quote means . . .

March 27

People say that what we're all seeking is the meaning of life . . . I think that what we're really seeking is the experience of being alive.
Joseph Campbell

Writing: Things I love about my unique, special life:

March 28

The greatest lesson in life is to know that even fools are right sometimes.
Winston Churchill

Writing: When have I used labels and epithets to categorize people and how has that served me? Was I ever harsh or dare I say wrong in calling someone a fool?

March 29

I take a simple view of life:
keep your eyes open and get on with it.
Laurence Olivier

Writing: I see with my wide open eyes:

March 30

Joking is undignified: that is why it's so
good for one's soul.
C.K. Chesterton

Writing: It makes me chuckle and chortle
to think of the time when . . .

March 31

Gratitude unlocks the fullness of life. It turns what we have into enough, and more. It turns denial into acceptance, chaos to order, confusion to clarity. It can turn a meal into a feast, a house into a home, a stranger into a friend. Gratitude makes sense of our past, brings peace for today, and creates a vision for tomorrow.
Melody Beattie

Writing: Today's oops list:

Today's gratitude list:

April 1

You can only be young once. But you can always be immature.

Dave Barry

Writing: Ways I can explore my inner silliness:

April 2

All mankind is divided into three classes:
those that are immovable,
those that are movable,
and those that move.
Benjamin Franklin.

Writing: What moves me? What positions am I staunchly unshakeable about? How would it feel to take the opposing argument and pretend I believe it?

April 3

The curious paradox is that when I accept
myself just as I am, then I can change.
Carl Rogers

Writing: Carl Rogers, who died in 1987 at
the age of 85 is a founder of humanistic
"client-centered" psychology. The above
quotation appears in his 1961 book for
psychotherapists, *On Becoming a Person*. So,
what does it mean to "become a person"
and how damn hard is it for me to "accept
myself just as I am"?

April 4

It's never too late to be what you might
have been.
George Eliot

Writing: If I were eighteen again, what
would I study? What would I choose to do?

75

April 5

If you want to make an apple pie from scratch, you must first create the universe.
Carl Sagan

Writing: Oh, hell, I've still been feeling . . . about . . . Maybe if I write about it I'll feel better.

April 6

Happiness is realizing that nothing is too important.
Antonio Gala

Writing: How can I play and laugh more?

April 7

Just as a cautious businessman avoids
investing all his capital in one concern, so
wisdom would probably admonish us also
not to anticipate all our happiness from one
quarter alone.
 Sigmund Freud

Writing: How's my life balance been doing?
Am I spending too much time on . . . ?
What do I want to make more time for?

April 8

When we remember we are all mad, the
mysteries disappear and life stands
explained.
Mark Twain

Writing: So, I may not be the easiest person
to live with. How can I make a small
difference in the lives of the people I'm
closest to this week?

April 9

Because things are the way they are,
things will not stay the way they are.
Bertolt Brecht

Writing: Just for today I can . . .

April 10

How can we ever hope to grasp the deeper
possibilities of life, and lead invigorated or
meaningful days, if we're all dashing around
nonstop like water bugs on the surface of a
swirling river?
Robert K. Cooper

Writing: Whew, whoosh, today's writing
can be a chance to breathe and observe how
my whole stomach and ribcage expands and
contracts with each breath. Gratitudes for
today are:

April 11

You will either step forward into growth or
you will step back into safety.
Abraham Maslow

Writing: A daring risky wonderful thing I
did recently was . . .

A daring, risky, wonderful thing I want to
do is . . .

April 12

Happiness is to be found along the way, not at the end of the road, for then the journey is over and it is too late. Today, this hour, this minute is the day, the hour, the minute for each of us to sense the fact that life is good, with all of its trials and troubles, and perhaps more interesting because of them.
Robert R. Updegraff

Writing: What can I learn from the metaphoric flies and mosquitoes and poisonous snakes in my life? How can I become less annoyed with them?

April 13

If we listened to our intellect, we'd never have a love affair. We'd never have a friendship. We'd never go into business, because we'd be cynical. Well, that's nonsense. You've got to jump off cliffs all the time and build your wings on the way down.
Ray Bradbury

Writing: What do I simply absolutely deserve this week?

April 14

When we ask for advice, we are usually looking for an accomplice.
Marquis de la Grange

Writing: If I could pick up the phone and pour my heart out and ask for advice from anyone in the world, who would I call and what would that person say to me in response to my words?

April 15

Being rich isn't about money. Being rich is a state of mind. Some of us, no matter how much money we have, will never be free enough to take time to stop and eat the heart of the watermelon. And some of us will be rich without ever being more than a paycheck ahead of the game.
Harvey Mackay

Bonus quote:
What's the use of happiness?
It can't buy you money.
Comedian Henny Youngman

Writing: How healthy or unhealthy are my attitudes and behaviors around money? What do I need to change in my relationship with holding onto, saving, and spending money?

April 16

There is nothing in the universe with the
power to hold the human mind in painful
captivity except for the cage it builds for
itself out of its own mistaken thinking.
Guy Finley

Writing: Maybe if I saw the world with
. . . 's eyes I'd have a different outlook. If
I want to find a lost contact lens I have to
crawl around on the carpet. If I want to
consider how a nonagenarian or
quadriplegic sees the world, I might have to
slow my pace. How can I modify my
perspective or vantage point?

April 17

Sometimes I've believed as many as six impossible things before breakfast.
Lewis Carroll

Writing: "Impossible" things I can believe today:

April 18

There's no point in being grown up if you can't be childish sometimes.
Doctor Who

Writing: What child or children can I carefully observe? Is there someone I can tickle today? How can I be childish with the adults in my environment?

April 19

It is only possible to live happily ever after-
on a day-to-day basis.
Margaret Bonnano

Writing: What's my happily-ever-after
story?

April 20

Remind yourself often:
All thoughts create.
Then decide what it is
that you want to make.
Lee J. Jampolsky

Writing: In a five-hour creative window of
time with a vast supply of materials, what
would I make? What work of art does my
mind's eye see?

April 21

Each of us makes his own weather,
determines the color of the skies in the
emotional universe which he inhabits.
Fulton J. Sheen

Writing: April's a month for talking about
the weather. Why and when do I talk to
people around me about safe, non-
controversial topics? How do I feel about
such small talk? Do I use it to keep peace,
to change subjects? Do I avoid it? Am I
snobbish about small talk?

April 22

You are a living magnet. What you attract
into your life is in harmony with your
dominant thoughts.
Brian Tracy

Writing: What am I seeking to attract more
of in my life and how am moving toward
getting what I want? [Or am I simply
believing in the "law of attraction" and not
taking any action?]

April 23

If we try hard to bring happiness to others,
we cannot stop it from coming to us also.
To get joy, we must give it, and to keep joy,
we must scatter it.
John Templeton

Writing: . . . did such a nice thing for me
recently. Maybe I can pass it on?

April 24

We might feel that somehow we should try
to eradicate these feelings of pleasure and
pain, loss and gain, praise and blame, fame
and disgrace. A more practical approach
would be to get to know them, see how they
hook us, see how they color our perception
of reality; see how they aren't all that solid.
Pema Chödrön

Writing: Hooks:

April 25

At various times of life, we find ourselves
with a handful of blocks of different sizes
and shapes, out of which we can build some
aspect of life, and it behooves us to build it
as beautifully as we can...
Isaac Asimov

Writing: A small list of people and things I
am blessed to have right now in my life:
[today's list can be about less obvious hings,
such as my esophagus, eyelashes, favorite
pillow, etc.]

April 26

Man cannot remake himself without
suffering for he is both the marble and the
sculptor.
Alexis Carrell

Writing: Let me just doodle a bit today,
doodle, squiggles and colors and shapes on
a full page and see what I get. And let me
remind myself that all of my feelings are
valid including sadness, anger, and misery.

April 27

You are searching for the magic key that
will unlock the door to the source of power;
and yet you have the key in your own hands,
and you may use it the moment you learn to
control your thoughts.
Napoleon Hill

Writing: What do I think really? Can I
learn to control my thoughts? Why and
when does my mind wander?

April 28

Loyalty to petrified opinion never yet broke
a chain or freed a human soul.
Mark Twain

Writing: If I took an opposing view of that
political or theological argument, what
points what would I make?

April 29

Have you realized that most of your
unhappiness in life is due to the fact that
you are listening to yourself instead of
talking to yourself?
 David Martin Lloyd-Jones

Writing: Ha, ha, ha, as if I could really
understand that complex little mind of
mine. Dear me, here are some words of
love:

April 30

There are two tragedies in life.
One is not to get your heart's desire.
The other is to get it.
George Bernard Shaw

Writing: Another thoughtful quotation,
what would be tragic if I had everything my
heart desired? What are some desires
dancing around in my heart and mind?

May 1

What if we smashed the mirrors and saw
our true face?
Elsa Gidlow

Writing: In *Henry VIII*, Shakespeare wrote
"All hoods make not monks." (Long
before, in 1387, Chaucer wrote, "habit
maketh no monk" to be pedantic about it).
How, when and where do I pretend to be "a
monk"? When do I take the hood off?

May 2

The real voyage of discovery consists not in seeking landscapes, but in having new eyes.
Marcel Proust

Writing: Ode to my senses:

May 3

Let us not look back in anger or forward in fear but around in awareness
James Thurber

Writing: My surroundings. What's my favorite spot in my residence and what do I love about it? Where in my home can I make improvements?

May 4

No person is your enemy, no person is your friend, every person is your teacher.
Florence Scoval Shinn

Writing: Who am I still, still, STILL angry at? What can I learn from my displeasure and annoyance? What can I learn from *that* teacher in my life?

May 5

God gives us the nuts, but he does not crack them.
German proverb

Writing: What metaphors can I dream up? God made the lake, but he doesn't row the boat.

May 6

I am a nobody, and nobody is perfect;
therefore I am perfect.

Chocolate is good; life is good;
therefore chocolate is life.

Writing: Playing with language and silly
syllogisms.

May 7

Experience is what you get five minutes
after you need it.
Unknown

Writing: If only . . .

May 8

People often say that motivation doesn't
last. Well, neither does bathing - that's why
we recommend it daily.
Zig Ziglar

Writing: Today I feel motivated to . . .

May 9

Your diamonds are not in far distant
mountains or in yonder seas; they are in
your own backyard, if you but dig for them.
Russell H. Conwell
(quoted by Sarah Ban Breathnach)

Writing: There are Persian, Hassidic and
other legends of people who travel the
world to look for what they had all along.
In a way, it's also the story of the Buddha
who had a good life until he gave it all up to
develop his spirit. What treasures have I
overlooked in my searches for immediate
gratification or some illusive more and
more?

May 10

Every experience is a learning experience.
Every time we do something--win or lose--
we learn, we grow, we attain more
confidence and competence for the next
time.
Pat Williams, Basketball executive

Writing: Actions to take. A To-Do list to
really look at and cross off.

May 11

Pleasure is spread through the earth in stray
gifts to be cherished by whoever shall find.
William Wordsworth

Writing: I love . . .

May 12

Live out of your imagination, not your history.
Stephen R. Covey

Writing: Some future dreams, ideas, possibilities.

May 13

The bend in the road is not the end of the road...
UNLESS you refuse to make the turn.
Source unknown (found on a poster)

Writing: What does "resilience" mean to me?

May 14

What lies behind us,
And what lies before us,
Are tiny matters compared
To what lies within us.
Ralph Waldo Emerson

Writing: I am proud of myself. I showed
my strengths of character when I . . .

May 15

Sour, sweet, bitter, pungent, all must be tasted.
Chinese Proverb

Writing: What new experience can I engage in?

May 16

The longer one lives, the more one realizes that nothing is a dish for every day.
Norman Douglas

Writing: How have I been out of balance lately-- with which excesses and which lacks?

May 17

With an eye made quiet by the power of
harmony,   and the deep power of joy,
we see into the life of things.
William Wordsworth

Writing: How about a 5-7-5 syllable haiku
today in celebration of some tiny thing? Or
a simple reflection on "the life of things?"

May 18

You don't get harmony when everybody
sings the same note.
Doug Floyd

Writing: What opinion do I have of a show
or movie I saw recently? What's my
considered critique? Do I or should I watch
the world as a critical observer?

May 19

If we cannot now end our differences, at
least we can help make the world safe for
diversity.
John F. Kennedy

Writing: What does it mean to be a tolerant
person? How can I be more accepting of
people around me?

May 20

Everything you can imagine is real.
Pablo Picasso

You have your brush, you have your colors,
you paint paradise, then in you go.
Nikos Kazantzakis

Writing: What is revealed on my white
canvas?   What would be chipped away
from a huge block of marble if I were a
persevering, talented sculptor?

Alternative Writing: My opinions about
Picasso, 19th century art, Impressionism, etc.
When next will I spend time in an art museum?
How do I feel at museums? With whom would
I most like to meander around galleries or take
in a museum?

May 21

The miracle is this—the more we share,
the more we have.
Leonard Nimoy

Writing: What are my opinions about
generosity, charitable donations, tithing 10
% or hoarding?

May 22

The best place to find helping hands is at
the end of your own arms.
Swedish proverb

Writing: I can write out a little body scan.
What parts of my body ache for love and
attention?

May 23

The Possible's slow fuse is lit
By the Imagination.
Emily Dickinson

Writing: How would I imagine a wonderful
home? Workplace? Performance?

May 24

What if you slept, and what if in your sleep
you dreamed, and what if in your dream you
went to heaven and there you plucked a
strange and beautiful flower, and what if
when you awoke you had the flower in your
hand? Oh, what then?
Samuel Taylor Coleridge

Writing: Do I know what's real and true?
If I accept what he/she said about . . ., how
would that be for me?

May 25

Only a fool tests the depth of the water with both feet.
African proverb

Writing: When is it a good idea to throw caution to the wind? How and when do I need to be more cautious? What advice would I give to a young teenager today about risk taking and risk avoidance?

May 26

What we believe is based on our perceptions. What we perceive depends on what we look for. What we look for depends on what we think. What we think depends on what we perceive. What we perceive determines what we take to be true. What we take to be true is our reality.
Gary Zukav

Writing: Conceptions or misconceptions? How do I go about admitting that I was wrong?

May 27

Cats are intended to teach us that not
everything in nature has a function.
Garrison Keillor

Writing: What would *that* cat say if he/she
could talk?

May 28

Attitude is more important than the past,
than education, than money, than
circumstances, than what other people think
or say or do. It is more important than
appearance, giftedness, or skill. It will make
or break a company, a church, a home.
Charles Swindoll

Writing: And now I address the dragon or
devil   that's been attacking me: And then I'll
put on a different attitude.

May 29

Life moves on, whether we act as cowards or heroes. Life has no other discipline to impose, if we would but realize it, than to accept life unquestioningly. Everything we shut our eyes to, everything we run away from, everything we deny, denigrate, or despise, serves to defeat us in the end. What seems nasty, painful, evil, can become a source of beauty, joy, and strength, if faced with an open mind. Every moment is a golden one for him who has the vision to recognize it as such.
Henry Miller

Writing: Let me write about feelings and thoughts that have been bugging me or golden moments or simply do a free-association writing:

May 30

When you cease to dream, you cease to live.
Malcolm Forbes

Writing: Something I read recently that I
really loved was . . .

May 31

The greatest obstacle to discovery is not
ignorance — it is the illusion of knowledge.
Daniel J. Boorstin

Writing: Hey maybe I'll let my "opponent"
win the argument and just listen to what is
being said.
. . . 's point of view about . . .
is . . .

June 1

To see what is in front of one's nose
requires constant struggle.
George Orwell

Writing: The Yiddish writer Mendele
Mocher Seforim said a man can detect a
speck in another's hair, but can't see a fly on
the end of his own nose. When have I been
critical of another lately and how warranted
was my opinion and judgment?

June 2

Keep your face to the sun and you cannot
see the shadow.
Helen Keller

What we see depends mainly on what we look
for.
John Lubbock

Writing and tasks: A hymn to green and the
great outdoors. Get into nature, see green,
kiss a rose petal, hug a tree. Wake up and
say, "Good morning sun" or even "Hello
rain, we need you to make our world green."
But first I'll wax lyrical about what I love in
nature.

June 3

To be obliged to beg our daily happiness
from others bespeaks a more lamentable
poverty than that of him who begs his daily
bread.
Charles Caleb Colton

Writing: Who in all my life have I ever
blamed for my discontent? Have I fully
taken my power back and away from that
person or those people?

June 4

Be glad of life because it gives you the
chance to love, to work, to play, and to look
up at the stars.
Henry Van Dyke

Writing: "The fault dear Brutus lies in our
stars." (from *Julius Caesar*). Romeo and
Juliet were "star-crossed lovers". Ok, what
do I really think about astrology or fate or
"it's in the stars". Is anything or everything
pre-destined? How does my free will
determine my life?

June 5

Where the soul is full of peace and joy,
outward surroundings and circumstances
are of comparatively little account.
Hannah W. Smith

Writing: Soul checkup: Outside world
check-up: Have I been radiating serenity,
joy and benevolence lately or . . . ?

June 6

Fear is just excitement in need of an attitude
adjustment.
Russ Quaglia

Writing: I have recently felt fear around . .
How can I turn that feeling to my
good use?

June 7

Fear of failure will absolutely destroy you.
You will walk down the middle of the street.
You will never take chances. You never go
down the little side street that you look at
and say. "That looks interesting. But I don't
know that street. I'll stay right here and just
walk this straight line."
Jack Lemmon in *The Achievement Factors*

Writing: Today, I'll write the introduction
that the host of my favorite talk show will
make when I come out for my dream-
fulfilling 15-minute spot. "And now, please
welcome the amazing, the brilliant . . . "

June 8

There is a vitality, a life force, an energy, a quickening, that is translated through you into action, and because there is only one of you in all time, this expression is unique. And if you block it, it will never exist through any other medium and it will be lost.
Martha Graham

Writing: So, back to fate, do I have a sense of mission and purpose? What's driving my engine?

June 9

It's no good running a pig farm badly for thirty years while saying, "Really I was meant to be a ballet dancer." By that time, pigs will be your style.
Quentin Crisp

Writing: When I was a child, what did I want to be when I grew up? What ideas did I have about grown-ups?

June 10

Ideas are like rabbits. You get a couple and learn how to handle them, and pretty soon you have a dozen of them.
John Steinbeck

Writing: A lovely idea comes into my head to . . .

June 11

Yes, risk-taking is inherently failure-prone. Otherwise, it would be called sure-thing-taking.
Tim McMahon

Writing: What risks and challenges can I list that I can actualize during the next week?

June 12

The logic of worldly success rests on a fallacy—the strange error that our perfection depends on the thoughts and opinions and applause of other men. A weird life it is to be living always in somebody else's imagination, as if that were the only place in which one could become real.
Thomas Merton

Writing: Would I do anything different today or this year if I knew that nobody in the world was judging me or talking about me? If I were in a conversation with a child who'd been hurt by other children's taunting, what would I love to tell her?

June 13

An idealist is one who, on noticing that a rose smells better than a cabbage, concludes that it will also make a better soup.
H. L. Mencken

No pessimist ever discovered the secrets of the stars or sailed to an uncharted land or opened a new heaven to the human spirit.
Helen Keller

Writing: So how much am I an idealist, how much a realist, how much an optimist, how much a pessimist? Someone once said that the optimist builds the planes and the pessimist builds the parachutes, what do I do? I choose to be optimistic about . . .

June 14

If only we wanted to be happy, it would be easy; but we want to be happier than other people which is difficult, since we think them happier than they are.
Barron de Montesquieu

Writing: How much luxury is this! So many people in the world could never just sit around and write. What I love about sitting here in my favorite spot:

June 15

We forfeit three-fourths of ourselves to be like other people.
Arthur Schopenhauer

Writing: What I accept wholeheartedly about myself: What I love about myself:

June 16

Be patient toward all that is unresolved in your heart and try to love the questions themselves.
Rainer Maria Rilke

Writing: Did I ever answer that sophomoric question, "who am I"?   Have I found my identity?   Am I still searching?   Is it okay to have a midlife passage period that lasts for decades?

June 17

Risk! Risk Anything!
Care no more for the opinion of others, for those other voices. Do the hardest thing on earth for you. Act for yourself. Face the truth.
Katherine Mansfield

Writing: For me alone, I will . . . and I will look in the mirror and tell myself, . . .

June 18

We can't solve problems by using the same kind of thinking we used when we created them.
Albert Einstein

You won't dig an orange out of the mud or pick a potato from a tree.
Source unknown

Writing: I can appreciate potatoes for their potato-ness and oranges for their orange-ness and not try to compare one to another. Today I appreciate . . .

June 19

We are here and it is now. Further than that,
all knowledge is moonshine.
H.L. Mencken

Writing: Woo hoo, whoopee, calloo, callay,
oh frabjous day, I am so happy with my
present perspectives and capabilities:

June 20

A fool sees not the same tree that a wise
man sees.
William Blake

Writing: I can use all my senses in today's
writing and a few adjectives too just to
exercise my presence and use of language.
Here now is a description of . . .

June 21

My imagination makes me human and
makes me a fool; it gives me all the world
and exiles me from it.
Ursula K. Le Guin

Writing: Imagination play. What would my
bed say to me if it could talk? What would
the table, chairs, flies on the wall like to say?

June 22

Those who dream by day are cognizant of
many things which escape those who dream
only by night.
Edgar Allen Poe

Writing: Ok, okay I'll actually write my
fantasy down. What a fantastical dream I
can create with my words.

124

June 23

Creativity is allowing yourself to make mistakes. Art is knowing which ones to keep.
Scott Adams

Writing: When was the last time I cracked open one of those coffee table art books and studied the pictures? How do I feel when I look at works of art? Am I bored, inspired, baffled?

June 24

I long to accomplish a great and noble task,
but it is my chief duty to accomplish small
tasks as if they were great and noble.
Helen Keller

Writing: I don't have to consider
Sisyphusian the tasks of washing dishes, or
making beds that will be unmade the same
night. How can such repetitive tasks be
ennobling?

June 25

Life is a mirror and will reflect back to the
thinker what he thinks into it.
 Ernest Holmes

Writing: Mirror, mirror on the bathroom
wall, what do you want to reveal to me in
joy and love today?

June 26

Your present circumstances don't determine where you can go; they merely determine where you start.
Nido Qubein

Writing: Today I . . .

June 27

Begin today! No matter how feeble the light, let it shine as best it may. The world may need just that quality of light which you have.
Henry C. Blinn

Writing: What have I been procrastinating on lately? What plan can I write out for taking action?

June 28

Let us be silent, that we may hear the
whispers of the gods.
Ralph Waldo Emerson

Writing: Hello inner voice, what are you
telling me today?

June 29

Let us be grateful to people who make us
happy, they are the charming gardeners who
make our souls blossom.
Marcel Proust

Writing: Positive grateful thoughts I'm
putting into my head today are:

June 30

Imagination grows by exercise and contrary to common belief is more powerful in the mature than in the young.
W. Somerset Maugham

Writing: Green sky and blue trees, today I can play with my imagination and imagine a more ideal school or work or living environment or invent my own creatures like Dr. Seuss did or imagine alternate ways of gaining income for people who need to increase their financial reserves.
Hmmmmmm, imagine. . .

July 1

If you want a kinder world, then behave
with kindness; if you want a peaceful world,
make peace within.
Dan Millman

Writing: So here now I can pretend I have
lots of answers. How could I bring peace to
a troubling situation in my microcosm or in
the current political environment?

July 2

The best way to have a good idea is to have
a lot of ideas.
Linus Pauling

Writing: A list of things I would love to
learn more about:

July 3

Most people are more comfortable with old problems than with new solutions.
Anonymous

Writing: Okay journal, I admit it, I still do that annoying idiosyncratic behavior or time dawdler. Why is it a comfort and support to me? How much do I want to keep holding on to it?

July 4

It's so simple to be wise. Just think of something stupid to say and then don't say it.
Sam Levenson

Writing: How did I feel last time I held my mouth? Was I feeling stifled, frustrated, smug, smart, superior, empowered, complacent, absent, or dreamy?

July 5

The secret to success is sincerity.
Once you can fake that, you've got it made.
Jean Gieraudoux

Writing: When have I enjoyed being a
"fake"? What am I snobbish about?

July 6

Confirmational bias guarantees that you will
always see what you are looking for.
Dr. Pat Love

Writing: How have my prejudiced notions
impeded me? How have they helped me?

July 7

Consistency is the last refuge of the unimaginative.
Oscar Wilde

Writing: What a great prerogative to be able to change my mind and be inconsistent. How accepting am I of others when they also change their minds or cancel appointments with me?

July 8

To aim at the best and to remain essentially ourselves is one and the same thing.
Janet Erskine Stuart

Writing: How is my writing practice bringing me in line with my essential self? Am I showing my true self to the world? When am I not?

July 9

"Giving again"? I asked in dismay. "Must I
keep giving time and money away"?
"No" said the Angel piercing me through.
"Just give until God stops giving to you."
Anonymous, quoted in Susan Jeffers,
End the struggle and Dance with Life

Writing: How comfortable or
uncomfortable do I feel with words like
"divine", "mystical" and "fated"? When
have I felt that something happened in a
divine plan or extraordinarily coincidental
act of good fortune?

July 10

The only joy in the world is to begin.
Cesare Pavese

Writing: Today's a good day to begin:

July 11

In daily life, we must see that it is not
happiness that makes us grateful,
But gratefulness that makes us happy.
Brother David Stendel Ras

Writing: Check-in: how do I feel today?
How does my body feel?
Who do I want to talk to about my feelings
today?

July 12

The one unchangeable certainty is that
nothing is unchangeable or certain.
John F. Kennedy

Writing: What would I change if I were the
mayor of my town or leader of my country?

July 13

Every animal leaves traces of what it was;
man alone leaves traces of what he created.
Jacob Bronowski

Writing: What creations do I really love?
Today, I so appreciate:

July 14

Creativity is allowing yourself to make mistakes. Art is knowing which ones to keep.
Scott Adams

Writing: The lazy, hazy days of summer. Itsy bitsy polka-dot bikini. Musings on music and songs from when I was young and thought endless time was in front of me:

July 15

We are never deceived;
we deceive ourselves.
Goethe

Writing: Oh come on, am I still kidding
myself about . . . ?
Do I or should I tell people my age, my
vulnerabilities, my mistakes; how do I feel
about doing that, proud or embarrassed?
Maybe I don't have to reveal all things in
order to be happy. Have I ever lied about
my age or other details of who I am?   How
has self-deception been a visitor in my life?

July 16

People say that what we're all seeking is the meaning of life. . . I think that what we're really seeking is the experience of being alive."
Joseph Campbell

Writing: What is it that lets me feel most alive? Being out with people or being at a restaurant, cinema, or show or creating and producing and working? How can I be more alive today?

July 17

You have powers you've never dreamed of...
You can do things you've never thought you
could do. . . .There are no limitations in
what you can do...except the limitations. . .
of your own mind.
Darwin P. Kingsley

Writing: Oh goodness, not another super-
charged motivational quote. My mind is not
limitless and I feel like complaining today
about . . . Then I'll take my mind back to
feeling wonderful!

July 18

Courage is the capacity to confront what
can be imagined.
Leo Rosten

Writing: Someone said courage is fear with
wings or courage is doing the thing we're
afraid of, not acting without fear. Am I
afraid of death, destitution, loneliness,
illness? What fears do I carry inside me?
What do I most fear? Why?

July 19

Every morning, when we wake up, we have 24 brand new hours to live. What a precious gift! We have the capacity to live in a way that these 24 hours will bring peace, joy, and happiness to ourselves and others.
Thich Nhat Hanh

Writing: What smiles can I smile now as I write? What gifts can I relish in these 24 hours?

July 20

Walk as if you are kissing the Earth with your feet.
Thich Nhat Hanh

Writing: What's my reaction to this quote? What other analogies can I think of with "kissing"? How much can I love simply walking or using my feet today?

July 21

Music. . . will help dissolve your perplexities and purify your character and sensibilities, and in time of care and sorrow, will keep a fountain of joy alive in you.
Dietrich Bonhoeffer

Writing: My mid-summer music:

July 22

When you take charge of your life, there is no longer a need to ask permission of other people or society at large. When you ask permission, you give someone veto power over your life.
Geoffrey F. Abert

Writing: What annoys me about having to be a responsible adult? Yippee, what do I love about being an adult?

July 23

What we call reality is an agreement that
people arrived at to make life more livable.
Louise Nevelson

Writing: The celebrated British actress,
Maggie Smith, close to age 80 and loving
her work told an interviewer that it feels like
she's always eating breakfast.
Why do my days "fly by" and when does
time ever "drag"?

July 24

There are many things that will catch my
eye, but there are only a few that catch my
heart...it is those I consider to pursue.
Tim Redmond

Writing: What's in my heart and soul today?

July 25

Happiness grows at our own firesides, and
is not to be picked in strangers' gardens.
Douglas Jerrold

Writing: What do I love in my home?
What would I love to jettison?

July 26

Magic has often been thought of us the art
of making dreams come true; the art of
realizing visions. Yet before we can bring
birth to the vision we have to see it.
Starhawk

Writing: When have I felt magic, divinity,
providence or destiny at work in my life?
What visions have I seen realized as if by
magic or providence?

July 27

Life... It tends to respond to our outlook, to shape itself to meet our expectations.
Richard M. DeVos

Writing: Can I remove expectation and judgment and opinion from this day and simply observe?

July 28

He is happiest, be he king or peasant, who finds peace in his home.
Johann von Goethe

Writing: There's a saying that "the king and the pawn in the chess game both return to the same box." How am I a pawn and how and when and where am I a king or queen?

147

July 29

Life is like a landscape. You live in the midst of it, but can describe it only from the vantage point of distance.
Charles A. Lindbergh

Writing: What I know now and love knowing that I didn't know 10 years ago or 20 years ago:

July 30

If I have learnt anything, it is that life forms no logical patterns. It is haphazard and full of beauties which I try to catch as they fly by, for who knows whether any of them will ever return?
Dame Margot Fonteyn

Writing: Am I still grieving the loss of . . . ? I can write about that today. Alternatively, I can describe some beautiful something that's in my world today.

July 31

Living is not enough. One must have
sunshine, freedom, and a little flower.
Hans Christian Andersen

Writing: When do I seek and need
freedom? When am I burdened by others?
When am I joyfully dependent on other
souls?

August 1

Life is denied by lack of attention, whether
it be to cleaning windows or trying to write
a masterpiece.
Nadia Boulanger

Writing: What will I pay more attention to
in August?

August 2

People take different roads seeking
fulfillment and happiness. Just because
they're not on your road doesn't mean
they've gotten lost.
H. Jackson Brown

Writing: My road with all the weeds and
thorns is the right one for me.

August 3

Time is the coin of your life. It is the only
coin you have, and only you can determine
how it will be spent. Be careful lest you let
other people spend it for you.
Carl Sandburg

Writing: How will I spend my time today
and in the next few days with joy? What
time burdens can I take off of my
shoulders?

August 4

We may pass violets looking for roses.
We may pass contentment looking for
victory.
Ben Williams

Writing: How can I enjoy the hearty
carnations instead of bemoaning the delicate
wilted roses?

August 5

Happiness is as a butterfly which, when
pursued, is always beyond your grasp, but
which if you will sit down quietly, may alight
upon you.
Nathaniel Hawthorne

Writing: With which environment, comfort
clothes, and beverages are my moments of
peace and silence enhanced? How am I
doing at finding and relishing my quiet
time?

August 6

Happiness often sneaks through a door you didn't know you left open.
John Barrymore

Writing: Are there doors I need to open or metaphoric fields that need be planted?
Am I maximizing my opportunities for joy, wonder and happiness or is this a fallow time preparing for a new cultivation?

August 7

Money can't buy happiness, but it can make you awfully comfortable while you're being miserable.
Claire Booth Luce

Writing: A joke I enjoyed recently:

August 8

To put the world in order,
we must first put the nation in order.
To put the nation in order,
we must put the family in order;
To put the family in order,
we must cultivate our personal life;
and to cultivate our personal life,
we must first set our hearts right.
Confucius

Writing: How's my personal life doing?
Anyone I need to apologize to? Phone calls
to make? E-mails to write?

August 9

Music... will help dissolve your perplexities and purify your character and sensibilities, and in time of care and sorrow, will keep a fountain of joy alive in you.
Dietrich Bonhoeffer

Writing: My music:

August 10

You have a song that's yours, and it's a worthwhile song. It might only be a little song, but there are people out there who will like it.
Philip Toshido Sudo

Writing: Songs and associations:

August 11

The only way on earth to multiply happiness
is to divide it.
Paul Scherer

Writing: Whose world can I light up this
week and how will I do it?

August 12

To laugh is to risk appearing the fool.
To weep is to risk appearing sentimental.
To reach out for another is to risk
involvement.
To expose feelings is to risk exposing your
true self.
To place your ideas, your dream before a
crowd is to risk their loss.
To love is to risk not being loved in return.
To live is to risk dying. To hope is to risk
failure.
But risks must be taken because the greatest
hazard in life is to risk nothing.
If you risk nothing and do nothing,
you dull your spirit.
You may avoid suffering and sorrow, but
you cannot learn, feel, change, grow, love,
and live.
Chained by your attitude, if you risk are you
free.

Attributed to Leo Buscalgia, William A.
Ward, and others

Writing: Risks for now and for my future
self:

August 13

Great tranquility of heart is his who cares
for neither praise or blame.
Thomas a Kempis

Writing: Oh, to heck with that opinion or
remark, I can know deep in my soul that I
have great value just as I am. What do I
really love and value about myself?

August 14

Remember the five simple rules to be
happy:
1. Free your heart from hatred.
2. Free your mind from worries.
3. Live simply
4. Give more.
5. Expect less.
Source unknown

Writing: Are these "simple rules"?
Thoreau said, "Simplify, simplify, simplify."
What's my opinion?

August 15

The "what should be" never did exist, but people keep trying to live up to it. There is no "what should be," there is only what is.
Lenny Bruce

Writing: What "shoulds" did I learn in my childhood? How have I overcome them to become my own person?

August 16

Life can only be understood backwards, but it must be lived forward.
Soren Kierkegaard

Writing: Today, I will . . .

August 17

Happiness lies in the consciousness we have
of it,
and by no means in the way the future
keeps its promises.
George Sand

Writing: Present self:
Future self:

August 18

You can't have a light without a dark to
stick it in.
Arlo Guthrie

Writing: Remember that old joke about the
guy looking for a lost contact lens under a
street light t night. Explaining himself to a
passerby he says, well I lost it over there,
but it's too dark there to look. In what dark
corner of my life do I want to shine a light?

August 19

Genuine happiness consists in those
spiritual qualities of love, compassion,
patience, tolerance and forgiveness and so
on. For it is these which provide both for
our happiness and others' happiness.
The Dalai Lama

Writing: Oh, man oh man, how saintly do
I have to become? Goodness universe, give
me patience and tolerance RIGHT NOW!
Oh, all right, when have I been just a bit
intolerant both with myself and others
recently? What do I want to do to love and
help myself, not to mention others I've
annoyed?

August 20

A thing of beauty is a joy forever.
John Keats

Writing: A thing of beauty can be temporal
or permanent in my mind. What's beautiful
around me?

August 21

The sun does not shine for a few trees and
flowers, but for the wide world's joy.
Henry Ward Beecher

Writing: Blessings to the sun: Blessings to
the rain: Oh, and thank the lord for the air
conditioner. What have I been taking for
granted lately that I can really appreciate?

August 22

We meet ourselves time and again in a thousand disguises on the path of life.
Carl Jung

Writing: What are some compliments paid to me recently? What compliments can I give to those nearest and dearest or even those I work with?

August 23

Let a joy keep you.
Reach out your hands and take it when it
runs by.
Carl Sandburg

Writing: What living things or aspects of
nature become metaphors for my beautiful
life? Butterflies, rainbows, flowers, ladybugs
all might seem cliché but so what? What
metaphors can I write that begin: Life is
. . . or My life is . . .

August 24

The fact is always obvious much too late,
but the most singular difference between
happiness and joy is that happiness is a solid
and joy a liquid.
J.D. Salinger

Writing: What do these words mean to me:
joy, contentment, happiness?

August 25

With penetrating insight, the mystics will tell us that when we have a desire for a certain thing, a certain experience, and we fulfill that desire, the happiness we feel is not something given by that thing or experience; it is due to having no craving for a little while.
Eknath Easwaran

Writing: What cravings are gnawing at me?

August 26

To truly laugh, you must be able to take your pain and play with it.
Charlie Chaplin

Writing: "Oh no, my brain hurts" ran a line in a sketch from Monty Python. Try telling someone the second toenail on your left foot is aching and see what sort of sympathy you get. How can I laugh at physical and emotional ailments today?

August 27

There is talent, beauty, wonder, and inspiration in your midst right now. To pass it by is to miss the gift. To stop and breathe it in is to be the recipient of a miracle.
Alan Cohen

Writing: Oh yes, there are extraordinary, talented people in my world. But are there also some miserable people in my life? Do I want them there? Which joyful, happy fulfilled people do I want to spend more time with?

August 28

If your ship doesn't come in, swim out to it!
Jonathan Winters

Writing: What and who are on your boat and what is far, far away ashore?

August 29

It is not easy to find happiness in ourselves,
and it is not possible to find it elsewhere.
Agnes Repplier

Writing: Okay, oops, have I been a nag to
. . . about . . . ? What behaviors that
annoy me about another person would also
describe me?

August 30

I was angry with my friend
I told my wrath, my wrath did end
I was angry with my foe
I told it not, my wrath did grow.
William Blake

Writing: What's the difference between an
enemy and a friend?

August 31

If you ever find happiness by hunting for it, you will find it, as the old woman did her lost spectacles, safe on her own nose all the time.
Josh Billings

Writing: The speck on my nose really can be as easy to see as the fly on your face if I turn my vision in and go a little cross-eyed. How much time today can I devote to a little silence, meditation and soul searching, just for this day?

September 1

There is a kind of happiness and wonder that makes you serious.   It's too good to waste on jokes.
C. S. Lewis

Writing: A description of serious happiness and wonder.

September 2

Every now and then go away and have a
little relaxation. To remain constantly at
work will diminish your judgment. Go some
distance away, because work will be in
perspective and a lack of harmony is more
readily seen.
Leonardo DaVinci

Writing: A popular scheme for enhanced
productivity with computer or other office
work is work 25 minutes, then take a 5
minute physical movement break and repeat
throughout the hours of scheduled work.
Would a pattern like this help me? How
can I get some distance away and get some
perspective from the job or tasks that fill my
waking hours?

September 3

If the day and night be such that you greet
them with joy, and life emits a fragrance like
flowers and sweet-scented herbs, is more
elastic, more immortal - that is your success.
All nature is your congratulation, and you
have cause momentarily to bless yourself.
Henry David Thoreau

Writing: The beauties of nature that I can
explore and celebrate:

September 4

Shared joy is a double joy;
shared sorrow is half a sorrow.
Swedish proverb

A problem shared is a problem halved.
Folk wisdom

Writing: What do I want to share? I am
blessed by my relationship(s) with . . .
Maybe it's time for me to show my
appreciation.

September 5

True life is lived when tiny changes occur.
Leo Tolstoy

Writing: Hmmm, let's see, paint my
toenails purple, buy a super special
chocolate confection, phone my college
roommate whom I haven't spoken to in
years. What small spontaneous act can lift
my heart?

September 6

Can anything be so elegant as to have few
wants, and to serve them one's self?
Ralph Waldo Emerson

Writing: Do I want what someone else has
or what's being advertised? What wants do
I still have?

September 7

Happiness is not in our circumstance but in ourselves. It is not something we see, like a rainbow, or feel, like the heat of a fire. Happiness is something we are.
John B. Sheerin

Writing: Hooray, today I'm simply happy because . . .

September 8

This time, like all times, is a very good one, if we but know what to do with it.
Ralph Waldo Emerson

Writing: It's about time I engage in . . .

September 9

Only those who have learned the power of sincere and selfless contribution experience life's deepest joy: true fulfillment.
Anthony Robbins

Writing: I recently felt a sense of fulfillment when . . .

September 10

This is the true joy of life, the being used up
for a purpose recognized by yourself as a
mighty one; being a force of nature instead
of a feverish, selfish little clot of ailments
and grievances, complaining that the world
will not devote itself to making you happy. I
am of the opinion that my life belongs to
the community, and as long as I live, it is my
privilege to do for it what I can.
George Bernard Shaw

Writing: How do I relate my attitude and
opinion to Bernard Shaw's opinions?

September 11

Mirth is like a flash of lightning that breaks
through a gloom of clouds and glitter for
the moment. Cheerfulness keeps up a
daylight in the mind, filling it with steady
and perpetual serenity.
Samuel Johnson

Writing: Today I remember both tragedy
and joy and bless the clouds, the rain, the
sun and the daylight.

September 12

How simple it is to see that we can only be
happy now, and there will never be a time
when it is not now.
Gerald Jampolsky

Writing: The person who recently annoyed
the heck out of me also has some wonderful
qualities:

September 13

We are not going to change the whole
world, but we can change ourselves and feel
free as birds. We can be serene even in the
midst of calamities and, by our serenity,
make others more tranquil. Serenity is
contagious. If we smile at someone, he or
she will smile back. And a smile costs
nothing. We should plague everyone with
joy. If we are to die in a minute, why not die
happily, laughing?
Swami Satchidananda

Writing: I feel tranquil and serene
when I . . .

September 14

Just as a cautious businessman avoids
investing all his capital in one concern, so
wisdom would probably admonish us also
not to anticipate all our happiness from one
quarter alone.
Sigmund Freud

Writing: Lately I've been neglecting . . .
maybe now is the time to do something
about it.

September 15

Some people don't know where they want
to go but complain a lot about not getting
there. Decide not to be one of them.
Lee L. Jampolsky

Writing: When I talk about . . . , do other
people hear it as complaining? This time
I'll just *talk* about it here in my private
journal.

September 16

Thousands of candles can be lighted from a single candle, and the life of the candle will not be shortened. Happiness never decreases by being shared.
Buddha

Writing: Today I am/was happy because:

September 17

[Humanity] has unquestionably one really effective weapon—laughter. Power, money, persuasion, supplication, persecution—these can lift at a colossal humbug—push it a little—weaken it a little, century by century; but only laughter can blow it to rags and atoms at a blast. Against the assault of laughter nothing can stand.
Mark Twain

Writing: Who can I laugh with?

September 18

Embrace relational uncertainty. It's called
romance. Embrace spiritual uncertainty. It's
called mystery. Embrace occupational
uncertainty. It's called destiny. Embrace
emotional uncertainty. It's called joy.
Embrace intellectual uncertainty. It's called
revelation.
Mark Batterson

Writing: Surprise. Life is so full of
surprises.

September 19

I live my life in widening rings which spread
over earth and sky.
I may not ever complete the last one, but
that is what I will try.
Rainer Maria Rilke

Writing: I can imagine one far ripple that
words I said reached. I can behold one
small ring that actions I took spread out.

September 20

Too much of a good thing can be
wonderful.
Mae West

Writing: I can never have too much . . .

September 21

Happiness is a by-product of an effort to
make someone else happy.
Gretta Brooker Palmer

Writing: Yesterday I . . .

September 22

All our dreams can come true, if we have
the courage to pursue them.
Walt Disney

Writing: If I were feeling courageous this
week I would . . .

September 23

Joy is everywhere; it is in the earth's green
covering of grass, in the blue serenity of the
sky, in the reckless exuberance of spring, in
the severe abstinence of gray winter, in the
living flesh that animates our bodily frame,
in the perfect poise of the Human figure,
noble and upright, in living, in the exercise
of all our powers, in the acquisition of
knowledge; in fighting evils....
Joy is there everywhere.
Rabindranath Tagore

Writing: The sky, the change of seasons,
grass, trees . . . How am I feeling with
and on the earth and in nature today?

September 24

As soap is to the body,
so laughter is to the soul.
Yiddish Proverb

Writing: Today . . .

September 25

Happiness is not achieved by the conscious
pursuit of happiness; it is generally the by-
product of other activities.
Aldous Huxley

Writing: Am I balancing out how much
time I'm spending doing what I have to do
with doing what I love? Do I need to make
a change?

September 26

Intuitive responses are responses which
originate from joy.
Sylvia Clare

Writing: Breathe, breathe, what has my
intuition been hinting, whispering, shouting
at me in recent days? Does my intuition
suggest I take an action which my conscious
self is resisting? How can I get closer to
my deep intuitive understanding?

September 27

Earth's crammed with heaven.
Elizabeth Barrett Browning

Writing: Heaven, paradise, utter joy for
today would include . . .

September 28

No matter how much madder it may make
you, get out of bed forcing a smile. You may
not smile because you are cheerful; but if
you will force yourself to smile, you'll end
up laughing. You will be cheerful because
you smile. Repeated experiments prove that
when man assumes the facial expressions of
a given mental mood — any given mood —
then that mental mood itself will follow
Kenneth Goode

Writing: Okay, what do I see when I gaze
in the mirror and smile? Is it a true smile?
Is it forced? Am I seeing my beauty or my
flaws? How do I feel when I look at my
reflected smile and say, "Sweetheart, you're
beautiful. I love you."

September 29

Thousands of candles can be lighted from a
single candle, and the life
of the candle will not be shortened.
Happiness never decreases by being shared.
Buddha

Writing: Oh, to heck with Buddha, saints,
and "perfect people", I want to write about
some residual anger that's nagging at me
about . . .

Then I can light a candle, breathe and move
away from pain and anger and back into my
joyful gratitude.

September 30

Let us be grateful to people who make us happy; they are the charming gardeners who make our souls blossom.
Marcel Proust

Writing: To whom do I owe a word of thanks and how do I show him/her/them my gratitude?

October 1

The timeless in you is aware of life's timelessness; and knows that yesterday is but today's memory and tomorrow is today's dream.
Kahlil Gibran

Writing: Here I am with my writing time and my deep breathing and my gratitude for all the good things that surround me. I can move forward in this time and this place and feel my peace for the moment. My peace and serenity is nurtured and nourished by . . .

October 2

Happiness is not in the mere possession of money; it lies in the joy of achievement, in the thrill of creative effort.
Franklin D. Roosevelt

Writing: What creative endeavor has been satisfying me recently and how will I nurture the time to keep developing it?

October 3

Affection is responsible for nine-tenths of whatever solid and durable happiness there is in our lives.
C. S. Lewis

Writing and tasks for today: What attitudes did I learn about displays of affection from my childhood family members and how has that worked for me as an adult? How do I feel about people who are more or less publically affectionate than I am? Who would I love to hug today? What dog or cat can I show affection to today? How about doing some self affection—caressing our arms, cheeks, the backs of our necks, etc.?

October 4

Happiness is the meaning and the purpose
of life, the whole aim and end of human
existence.
Aristotle

Writing: Philosophic musings:

October 5

Happiness depends more on the inward
disposition of mind than on outward
circumstances.
Benjamin Franklin

Writing: My mind is my center for
happiness. How have I been managing
negative and destructive thinking lately?

October 6

Many people have a wrong idea of what
constitutes true happiness. It is not attained
through self-gratification, but through
fidelity to a worthy purpose.
Helen Keller

Writing: How do I rate and evaluate my
faithfulness in taking care of and standing
up for what's important to me?
A short inventory of my core values:

October 7

Plenty of people miss their share of
happiness, not because they never found it,
but because they didn't stop to enjoy it.

Setting a good example for children takes all
the fun out of middle age.

Both quotes are from William Feather

Writing: Today I'll simply slow down,
breathe and smile especially when . . .

October 8

The happiness of life is made up of minute
fractions—the little soon-forgotten charities
of a kiss, a smile, a kind look, a heartfelt
compliment in the disguise of a playful
raillery, and the countless other infinitesimal
of pleasurable thought and genial feeling.
Samuel Taylor Coleridge

Writing: I am deliciously happy that . . .

October 9

Sometimes our light goes out but is blown
into flame by another human being. Each
of us owes deepest thanks to those who
have rekindled this light.
Albert Schweitzer

Writing: Blessings to my candle kindlers:

October 10

Happiness is not a state to arrive at, but a
manner of traveling.
Margaret Lee Runbeck

Writing: I am thrilled with anticipation for
. . .

October 11

But what is happiness except the simple harmony between a man and the life he leads?
Albert Camus

Writing: The word, "harmony" gives me thoughts and feelings about:

October 12

Great joy, especially after a sudden change of circumstances, is apt to be silent, and dwells rather in the heart than on the tongue.
Henry Fielding

Writing: The blessings of silence:

October 13

On the whole, the happiest people seem to be those who have no particular cause for being happy except that they are so.
William R. Inge

Writing: A person I know who seems genuinely happy by nature is . . .

October 14

Happiness always looks small while you hold it in your hands, but let it go, and you learn at once how big and precious it is.
Maxim Gorky

Writing: Today is/was a good day because
. . .

October 15

Happiness consists in activity: such is the
constitution of our nature; it is a running
stream, and not a stagnant pool.
John M. Good

Writing: What happy things do I do at work
and home? What joyous activities do I do
outside of home and work? Is some re-
balancing in order?

October 16

The fear is worse than the pain.
Shannon Bahr

Writing: The last time I felt fear was . . .

October 17

Happiness is not in the mere possession of money; it lies in the joy of achievement, in the thrill of creative effort.
Franklin D. Roosevelt

Writing: I express my creativity when I . .

October 18

Precisely the least, the softest, lightest, a lizard's rustling, a breath, a flash, a moment - a little makes the way of the best happiness.
Frederich Nietzsche

Writing: Happiness is in the moments. Some of my favorites recently:

October 19

The really happy person is one who can
enjoy the scenery when on a detour.
Unknown

Writing: A small detail that gives / gave me
a huge smile:

October 20

It is only possible to live happily ever after
on a day to day basis.
Margaret Bonnano

Writing: When was the last time I felt the
catharsis of deep sadness and crying? How
did I get to the other side of the feelings?

October 21

One joy scatters a hundred griefs.
Chinese Proverb

Writing: How do I still experience the grief from the loss of . . . ? How do I continue to honor that memory and loss?

October 22

The grand essentials of happiness are: something to do, something to love, and something to hope for.
Allan K. Chalmers

Writing: I look forward with warm blessed anticipation to:

October 23

There is more to life than increasing its
speed.
Mahatma Gandhi

Writing: Today I'll breathe slowly and
appreciate . . .

October 24

Sometimes your joy is the source of your
smile, but sometimes your smile can be the
source of your joy.
Thich Nhat Hanh

Writing and task: How about smiling at and
to strangers and seeing what happens? How
about smiling the next time I'm on an
annoying phone call?

I can smile while I write this journal entry
about . . .

October 25

Everything has its wonders, even darkness and silence, and I learn whatever state I may be in therein to be content.
Helen Keller

Writing: Now is the time to . . .

October 26

The secret of happiness is not getting what you like, but liking what you get.
James M. Barrie

Writing: How did I want to be like Peter Pan back when I was a child? How do I still want to be a kid in NeverNeverLand?

October 27

What sane person could live in this world
and not be crazy?
Ursula K. LeGuin

Writing: Hooray for my insanity when I . . .

October 28

Most men pursue pleasure with such
breathless haste, that they hurry past it.
Soren Kierkegaard

Writing: Quick brainstorming lists—

Momentary Pleasures:

Sources of contentment:

Sources of happiness and joy:

October 29

Happiness is not a goal; it is a by-product.
Eleanor Roosevelt

Writing: How do I want to spend my days
differently than I am at present? How,
when and where am I still compromising
my time and what do I want to change, if
anything?

October 30

Don't walk in front of me, I may not follow.
Don't walk behind me, I may not lead.
Just walk beside me and be my friend.
Unknown (a popular poster in the 1970s)

Writing: When have I walked in front,
when behind, and when beside? Why and
why and why?

October 31

Happiness: an agreeable sensation arising
from contemplating the misery of another.
Ambrose Bierce, *The Devil's Dictionary*

Writing: I've come this far with writing and
contemplating. What does happiness mean
to me? Is it the immediate gratification of
free candy on Halloween? Is it feeling like
my life is better than someone else's i.e.,
"contemplating the misery of another"?
Could it be something much more
intangible?

November 1

Embrace fanaticism. Harness joie de vivre
by pursuing insane interests, consuming
passions, and constant sources of
gratification that do not depend on the
approval of others.
Elizabeth Wurtzel

Writing: When have I sought the approval
of another or been disturbed by someone's
disapproval? What would it feel like to
remove myself from thoughts of others'
disapproval?

November 2

The foolish man seeks happiness in the
distance; the wise grows it under his feet.
James Oppenheim

Writing: How much of my future happiness
do I need to plan for and how much can I
simply be in and with the present? What are
my priorities?

November 3

She took the leap and built her wings on the way down. When you reach for the stars you may not quite get one, but you won't come up with a handful of mud either.
Leo Burnett

Writing: When have I directed my gaze and my ambition very high and what happened? What would I do if I knew the outcome was assured? If I knew that at the end of 2 hours in the casino, I'd have the same $1000 that I started with, no matter what, how would I play?

November 4

Happiness is like a cloud. If you stare at it long enough, it evaporates.
Sarah Mclachlan

Writing: Okay, let's do a body check-in. Aches, pains, stiffness, flexibility, healthy eating? How am I doing? Are there messages my body wants me to know for today?

November 5

For most of life, nothing wonderful happens. If you don't enjoy getting up and working and finishing your work and sitting down to a meal with family or friends, then the chances are that you're not going to be very happy. If someone bases his happiness or unhappiness on major events like a great new job, huge amounts of money, a flawlessly happy marriage or a trip to Paris, that person isn't going to be happy much of the time. If, on the other hand, happiness depends on a good breakfast, flowers in the yard, a drink or a nap, then we are more likely to live with quite a bit of happiness.
Andy Rooney

Writing: Thanks for all the ordinary wonderful things in my life and maybe I'll even take a nap today or tomorrow or . . .

November 6

My life has been tapestry
of rich and royal hue,
an everlasting vision
of the ever-changing view.
Carole King

Writing: Hey, how about a change-up and
writing a limerick or a rhyme today? I don't
have to be a songwriting master like Carole
King to bring a smile to my face with a little
rhyming. I can try a little whimsy or even
autobiography:

Roses are red, violets are blue,
I love my computer,
It gives me lots to do.

I know a girl who lives far away
In a land where bad news comes to play
She ignores it all and starts to write
About peace and joy into the night,
While smiling silly day after day.

November 7

Happiness isn't something you experience;
it's something you remember.
Oscar Levant

Writing: How often do I visit my favorite
memories? A lovely memory I can enjoy
while writing today:

November 8

Happiness is when what you think, what
you say, and what you do are in harmony.
Mahatma Gandhi

Writing: Harmony??? How have my
alignment and integrity been lately? Are
there phone calls, apologies, actions that beg
to be done in order to restore my harmony?

November 9

If only we'd stop trying to be happy,
we could have a pretty good time.
Edith Wharton

Writing: Woo hoo, maybe I'll just laugh
raucously for no reason and not care if the
world thinks me a fool. What purely fun
thing can I do in the next 24 hours?

November 10

T-shirts:
The best vitamin to be a happy person is B1

Life is short, eat dessert first (also a motto
of an ice cream parlor)

Jumping for joy is good exercise.

Writing: If I wrote or wore a phrase on a t-
shirt, it might be . . .

November 11

Laughter is wine for the soul - laughter soft,
or loud and deep, tinged through with
seriousness - the hilarious declaration made
by man that life is worth living.
Sean O'Casey

Writing: What person in my life could use
a dose of humor? How and when will I try
to amuse the curmudgeon?   Oh, and of
course I'll practice my bottomless
compassion at the stick-in-the-mud's
miserable life too, hee, hee, hee, well, maybe
a little after the tickle torture finishes.

November 12

It is only when the mind is free from the old that it meets everything anew, and in that there is joy.

Jiddu Krishnamurti

Writing: Let's see, something new, a different route to the same destination, a new flavor to taste,. Muse, muse, muse. What's new? A new answer to a mundane question.

November 13

What the caterpillar calls a tragedy,
the Master calls a butterfly.
Richard Bach

Writing: Remember that Diana Ross song,
"upside down and inside out, boy you turn
me". Today I'll write and look from a whole
different perspective. Maybe I'll turn myself
into a fly on the wall or a puppy lurking
under the dining table and tell the story
from the animal's point of view.   Or, what
would the clock say about my early morning
routines and rituals? How can I re-tell the
narrative in a whole different voice and just
for fun?

November 14

Time spent laughing is time spent with the
gods.
Japanese Proverb

Writing: Nerts, nuts, nuisances, niggles and
piggles, I'm still letting that *junk* about . . .
get into my head. Maybe if I spread it out
here in my journal I can get it out of my
head.

November 15

A smile starts on the lips, a grin spreads to
the eyes, A chuckle comes from the belly;
But a good laugh bursts forth from the soul,
Overflows, and bubbles all around.
Carolyn Birmingham

Writing: Free, free, freedom to spend time
with my journal and my mind today, what's
flowing from my pen today? Maybe a
picture or something unexpected?

November 16

Some people complain because the roses
have thorns; I am happy that the thorns
have roses.
Alphonse Karr

Writing: What is the place of pessimism
and optimism and positive outlook in my
life? Is my nature naturally optimistic?

November 17

Life is too short to be little.
Benjamin Disraeli

Writing: Is there some little grudge or anger
I could diffuse?

November 18

Happiness is having a scratch for every itch.
Ogden Nash

Here are some more samples from the late
great phrase turner Ogden Nash:

You never get any fun out of the things
you haven't done.

There is only one way to achieve happiness
on this terrestrial ball,
and that is to have either a clear conscience
or none at all.

The only people who should really sin are
the people who can sin and grin.

Writing: How do I feel about conscience
and sin? What itches do I still have to
scratch?

November 19

My advice to you is not to inquire why or whither, but just enjoy your ice cream while it's on your plate.
Thornton Wilder

Writing: A play or movie that gives me warm memories. Which character did I identify with? Why did I love this show or movie?

November 20

There is no one luckier than he who thinks himself so.
German proverb

Writing: Hooray, how lucky am I to have . . .

November 21

Pleasure is spread through the earth
In stray gifts to be claimed by whoever shall
find.
William Wordsworth

Writing: How can I assert my wants and
needs this week in a way that will bring me
pleasure and maybe also transmit it to
someone else.

Bonus task: Maybe I need more touch,
hugs and caresses in my life. Can I ask
someone for a massage or pure affection
this week? What pets or people can I hug
more often?

November 22

You will never be happy if you continue to
search for what happiness consists of.
You will never live if you are looking for the
meaning of life.
Albert Camus

Writing: How much am I living in the
present? Am I still worried about stuff in
the future? Am I caught up in financial or
health worries?

November 23

Slow down, simplify and be kind.
Naomi Judd

Writing: Have I become a softer, kinder
person? Are the people around me kind?

November 24

The monkeys solved the puzzle simply
because they found it gratifying to solve
puzzles. They enjoyed it. The joy of the task
was its own reward.
Daniel H. Pink (yes, he's talking about real
experiments with monkeys.)

Writing: What task such as cooking or
writing do you do mainly for its own reward
and not for income or fame? What do you
love about "the joy of the task"?

November 25

A man's as miserable as he thinks he is.
Seneca

Two prisoners looked out through the bars;
One saw mud and the other stars.
Source unknown

Writing: What "prisons" have I been in
during my life? How (miserable or joyful)
do I want to choose to be today?

November 26

If you haven't made any mistakes lately, you
must be doing something wrong.
Susan Jeffers, *Feel the fear and Do it anyway*

Writing: I celebrate my humanity. It was
okay when I said or did *that thing*. Today I
lovingly forgive myself.

November 27

Joy is not incidental to the spiritual experience; it is vital.
Rabbi Nachman of Breslov

Writing: How much joy, laughter, silliness and pure fun do I really have in my life? Am I getting my fill?

November 28

Even a happy life cannot be without a measure of darkness, and the word happy would lose its meaning if it were not balanced by sadness. It is far better to take things as they come along with patience and equanimity.
Carl Jung

Writing: Okay, okay, joy, shmoy, happiness, schmappiness. I can be still and feel that I'm not happy about every area in my life, but I can accept with equanimity that which I cannot change.
What's been hard for me to accept lately?

November 29

If you can walk, you can dance.
If you can talk, you can sing.
Zimbabwean proverb

A person can drop dead even while singing.
But that's no reason to stop singing.
Marty Rubin

Writing: What's my song for today?
Can I sing it without regard to the sound of
my voice or who might hear?

November 30

Happiness makes up in height for what it
lacks in length.
Robert Frost

Writing: Life is so full of ups and downs.
What's been bringing me down lately?

December 1

"Either you will
go through this door
or you will not go through.
...
The door itself
makes no promises.
It is only a door."

Adrienne Rich

Writing: One of my simplest easiest joys
has been playing at anthropomorphism and
saying things like, "these shoes don't want
me to wear them today" or telling my son
that the toothbrush is thankful that he's
brushed every tooth so carefully. What
would my refrigerator, computer, shoes and
doors have to say to me today if they could
talk?

December 2

Every now and then,
when the world sits just right,
a gentle breath of heaven
fills my soul with delight...

Happiness and sadness run parallel to each
other.
When one takes a rest, the other one tends
to take up the slack.
Both quotes are from Hazelmarie Elliott

Writing: Today's a lovely day for me to try
my hand at a short verse.

December 3

The happiness of most people is not ruined by great catastrophes or fatal errors, but by the repetition of slowly destructive little things.

Ernest Dimnet

Writing: What more in my life can I delegate to others? What can I eject from my daily doings?

December 4

Get this if you get anything, you are *not* what you do.
If you are what you do, when you don't, you aren't. Your value comes from yourself and your very existence.
 Wayne Dyer

Writing: I am beautiful valuable person in this universe.
Today I observe and affirm . . .

December 5

Nobody really cares if you're miserable,
so you might as well be happy.
Cynthia Nelms

Writing: Ah, you know that person who is
addicted to suffering or at least talks about it
all the time. What mind games can I play to
enjoy the time my sense of obligation
requires me to be with him or her? And of
course, can I minimize the frequency and
duration of my contact without being too
offensive or feeling guilty about it?

December 6

Happiness is like a butterfly which, when pursued, is always beyond our grasp, but, if you will sit down quietly, may alight upon you.
Nathaniel Hawthorne

Writing: How about drawing some colorful butterflies just for fun today? What metaphoric butterflies would I like to land on me this week?

December 7

Precisely the least, the softest, lightest, a lizard's rustling, a breath, a flash, a moment - a little makes the way of the best happiness.
Frederich Nietzsche

Writing: What itsy bitsy observation in my writing will give me some a moment of happiness?

December 8

I would rather be ashes than dust! I would
rather that my spark should burn out in a
brilliant blaze than it should be stifled by
dry rot. I would rather be a superb meteor,
every atom of me in magnificent glow, than
a sleepy and permanent planet. The proper
function of man is to live, not to exist. I
shall not waste my days in trying to prolong
them. I shall use my time."
Jack London

Writing: Oh alright, I'll muster up my
energy. I'll do something marvelous and a
bit daring. Let's see . . .

December 9

When humor goes, there goes civilization.
Erma Bombeck

Writing: What has made me laugh recently?
What did I say or do that made someone
else laugh?

December 10

Remember happiness doesn't depend upon
who you are or what you have; it depends
solely upon what you think.
Dale Carnegie

Writing: Too much outside news in my life,
maybe I need to shut down and tune out the
world. What's on the inside?

December 11

Evil (ignorance) is like a shadow--it has no real substance of its own; it is simply a lack of light. You cannot cause a shadow to disappear by trying to fight it, stamp on it, by railing against it, or any other form of emotional or physical resistance. In order to cause a shadow to disappear, you must shine light on it.
Shakti Gawain

Writing: Here's a task I learned from fellow journal-keeper, Sandy Grason. Set a timer for 10 minutes and sit down to write with no editorial pause, without letting your pen go idle. Now, finish this sentence and keep going:
"I really don't want to write about . . ."

December 12

The world is but canvas to our imaginations.
Henry David Thoreau

Writing: In Hamlet, Shakespeare used the phrase, "in my mind's eye" to explain where *Hamlet* had seen his dead father, and in Sonnet 113, Shakespeare wrote, "since I left you, mine eye is in my mind". Shakespeare also coined the expression, "love is blind" in *The Merchant of Venice*. What does my mind "see" today? Where and how am I still blind? What blindspots are there inside my mind?

December 13

Man is fond of counting his troubles, but he does not count his joys. If he counted them up as he ought to, he would see that every lot has enough happiness provided for it.
Fyodor Dostoevsky

Writing: Woo hoo, I can feel phenomenally happy because . . .

December 14

Guard well your spare moments.
They are like uncut diamonds. Discard them
and their value will never be known.
Improve them and they will become the
brightest gems in a useful life.
Ralph Waldo Emerson

Writing: When will I take some "me" time
this week and what splendid scrumptious
self-love would I love to do?

December 15

Life is not lost by dying.
Life is lost minute by minute,
day by dragging day,
in all the thousand small uncaring ways.
Stephen Vincent Benet

Writing: Time check. How have I been
managing my time lately? How can I
modify my efficiency? How and when can I
find more time to play?

December 16

Dreaming permits each and every one of us to be quietly and safely insane every night of our lives.
William Dement

Writing: Sane dreams:
Insane dreams:

December 17

Know your lines and don't bump into the furniture.
Spencer Tracy,
on how to succeed as an actor

Writing: When I feel grumpy and tired, I need to "suit up and show up". When does this advice help me and when do I still want to curl up in bed and disappear? What makes me want to "lie in" as they say in England?

December 18

As you go the way of life
you will see a great chasm.
Jump.
It is not as wide as you think.
Native American proverb

Writing: The last time I took a leap of faith,
what did I do and how did it turn out?

December 19

If the future road loom ominous or
unpromising, and the road back uninviting,
then we need to gather our resolve and,
carrying only the necessary baggage, step off
that road into another direction.
Maya Angelou

Writing: Oh to heck with what . . . thinks,
I will not attend to those opinions
about . . .

December 20

When you're really happy, the birds chirp
and the sun shines even on cold dark winter
nights - and flowers will bloom on a barren
land.
Terri Guillemets

Writing: Quiet, still, breathe, breathe, what
creative energy fills my stillness while I write
on this December day?

December 21

People don't notice whether it's winter or
summer when they're happy.
Anton Chekhov

Writing: Beautiful day. Somewhere on the
planet it's snowing and somewhere on the
planet sun lovers are frolicking on a beach.
I can love this day simply because . . .

December 22

Pleasure is very seldom found where it is
sought. Our brightest blazes are commonly
kindled by unexpected sparks.
Samuel Johnson

Writing: I see sparks in my mind
when I think of . . . and I can ignite them
into a warming flame when I . . .

December 23

Happiness cannot be traveled to, owned,
earned, worn or consumed. Happiness is the
spiritual experience of living every minute
with love, grace and gratitude.
Denis Waitley

Writing: Okay I'll write another gratitude
list because it brings me joy, but first I want
to vent about . . .

December 24

Real happiness is cheap enough, yet how
dearly we pay for its counterfeit.
Hosea Ballou

Writing: Material goods and gifts are not
the source of my happiness. I am happy
when I . . .

December 25

Happiness quite unshared can scarcely
be called happiness; it has no taste.

I would always rather be happy than
dignified.

Both quotes come from Charlotte Bronte

Writing: How great it is to be amongst
people with whom I can be undignified.
And what a great gift and blessing it is to say
from the heart, "thank you."
I am thankful for . . .

December 26

Don't go through life, grow through life.
Eric Butterworth

Writing: Today I'll choose to learn
in the area of . . .

December 27

If you observe a really happy man you will
find him building a boat, writing a
symphony, educating his son, growing
double dahlias in his garden, or looking for
dinosaur eggs in the Gobi desert. He will
not be searching for happiness as if it were a
collar button that has rolled under the
radiator. He will not be striving for it as a
goal in itself. He will have become aware
that he is happy in the course of living life
twenty-four crowded hours of the day.
W. Beran Wolfe

Writing: I am going to devote time to the
pure joy   of   . . . -ing
My small plan for doing what I love:

December 28

Comparison is the death of joy.
Mark Twain

Comparison is the thief of joy.
Theodore Roosevelt

Writing: I will appreciate my inner being
today and not compare myself with anyone
else's external appearance of well-being. My
universe is perfect for me even when I lapse
into argumentativeness, grumpiness or some
other lousy mood.   I'm going to just write
out that grumpiness and the good feelings
will take over.   Thank you, universe.

December 29

For every ailment under the sun,
there is a remedy or there is none.
If there be one try to find it.
If there be none, never mind it.
17th century nursery rhyme

Writing: I don't need to escape into gin or
vodka in order to revel with my fellow
party-goers, I can enjoy being in the
moment without altering my mind too
much. Nevertheless, if I choose to imbibe
or ingest a lot of sugar calories at this time
of year, I'll do it with gusto and active
choice. I will cultivate my practice of self-
awareness when I engage in social events.
What choices will I make in the next few
days?

December 30

You have brains in your head
and feet in your shoes.
You can steer yourself any direction you
choose.
You're on your own and you know what
you know.
And you are the one who'll decide
where to go.
Dr. Seuss

You had the power all along my dear.
Glinda the Good Witch
(from *The Wizard of Oz*, of course)

Writing: Yippee I am the one who's
pedaling the bicycle and how wonderful that
I am able to do it.   I can even ride tandem
and let God do the steering, but still I will
keep on pedaling no matter what the
destination.
What other metaphors can I come up with,
e.g., holding the reins, piloting the plane
. . .?

December 31

The world is round and the place which may seem like the end may also be the beginning.
Ivy Baker Priest

The end of all our exploring will be to arrive where we started and know the place for the first time.
T.S. Eliot

Writing: Circles and cycles guide my days when I look at them. How have I grown this year? How has my rating of subjective well-being changed (on a scale of 1-10, am I happier today than I was a year ago)? What small impacts have been made in my life through reading, writing, breathing, and living another year on earth?

∞∞∞∞∞∞∞∞∞∞∞∞∞∞∞∞∞∞

When you've got the muse

Here are some additional writing prompts when you want a substitute or feel a bit freer, more whimsical or creative. Some of these would be interesting dinner table conversation topics (along with your chosen favorites from the other 366).

1. What living or dead famous person would you like to have a conversation with and what would you talk about?
2. What fictional character would you like to have a conversation with and what would you talk about?
3. Who would you invite to sit down together for dinner if you could include 6-10 people living, dead, fictitious or real? What conversation topics would be broached?

4. What sentimental items would you take out of your home if you had time to grab 3 things in addition to your tangible valuables before your home was destroyed in fire? Why did you choose those 3 things?

5. What would you like to change about the life or personality of one of your relatives? How would that person feel about such a change?

6. How will people in 2065 describe and remember the decade and events we're living in right now?

7. What's your worst memory from a holiday family gathering?

8. What did you love about family celebrations when you were a child?

9. What did the fly on the wall say to another fly on the wall while witnessing . . .?

10. What will people say about you ten years from now? How will you describe your last 10 years?

11. If you could be anyone in the world for 24 hours but not yourself, who would you be and how would that day go for you?
12. Write in God's voice and explain why calamities have happened in human history.
13. Write in God's voice and describe the changes that will come into the world.
14. What would you like to see invented in your lifetime?
15. When was the last time you couldn't find the "right" words to say? What do you wish you had said or done?
16. How might your life have developed if you had made one single different decision when you were a teenager?
17. Write about a favorite memory from before you were 13.
18. Write about a favorite memory from your years as a teenager.
19. Write about a time when you were terrified.
20. What are your most secret "bad" habits and how much do you relish them?

21. Describe your favorite place from childhood.　Write with all of your five senses—what did it look, sound, smell, taste and feel like when you were in that special place?

22. If you could live in a different historic time period, when would that be? Write about that age?

23. Write out the entire dialogue between you and your imaginary friend who is feeling completely demoralized and depressed.

24. Be assertive . How many different ways can you decline an invitation without using the word, "no"?

25. Who was your first love? Write about that time? How would it be now if the two of you were stuck alone snow-stormed in a cottage for a weekend?

Appendix 1
Folk Wisdom

English language traditions comprise so many different cultures and sayings that we can often find someone else's words to say what we want to say. Obviously I love this or I wouldn't have compiled all those quotations.

I'd love to say I compiled this list of contradictory sayings but it was a handout that was used in teaching English as a foreign language many years ago, and I don't know who created it. You can choose whichever expression you want to back up your personal belief systems and arguments. Consider journaling about opinions or examples or stories to support any of these old adages.

1. You can't tell a book by its cover.
   Or
   Where there's smoke, there's fire.
2. He who hesitates is lost.
   Or
   Haste makes waste.
3. You can't teach an old dog new tricks.
   Or
   It's never too late to learn.
4. If at first you don't succeed, try, try again.
   Or
   Don't throw good money after bad.
5. There's always tomorrow.
   Or
   Never put off till tomorrow what you can do today.
6. Variety is the spice of life.
   Or
   A rolling stone gathers no moss.
7. Many hands make light work.
   Or
   Too many cooks spoil the soup.

8. An ounce of prevention is worth a pound of cure.

   Or

   Don't cross that bridge until you come   to it.

9. The grass is always greener on the other side of the fence.

   Or

   There's no place like home.

10. Beauty is only skin deep.

    Or

    Beauty is as beauty does.

11. It never rains but it pours

    Or

    Every cloud has a silver lining.

12. Out of sight out of mind.

    Or

    Absence makes the heart grow fonder.

13. The early bird catches the worm.

    Or

    All things come to he who waits.

14. Do as I say not as I do.

    Or

    Actions speak louder than words.

15. A bird in the hand is worth two in the bush.

    Or

    Hitch your wagon to a star.
16. Never look a gift horse in the mouth.

    Or

    All that glitters is not gold.
17. Quit while you're ahead.

    Or

    Nothing ventured, nothing gained.

Appendix 2
Writers on writing

Of course you can find an endless supply of quotes on the great internet, but here are a few that could be related to journal writing.

There is no greater agony than bearing an untold story inside you.
> Maya Angelou

If my doctor told me I had only six minutes to live, I wouldn't brood. I'd type a little faster.
> Isaac Asimov

A word after a word after a word is power.
> Margaret Atwood

A word is dead
When it is said
Some say
I say it just begins
To live that day.
> Emily Dickinson

Writers live twice.
> Natalie Goldberg

Writing is not necessarily something to be ashamed of, but do it in private and wash your hands afterwards.
> Robert A. Heinlein

My aim is to put down what I see and what I feel in the best and simplest way I can tell it.
> Ernest Hemingway

Prose is architecture, not interior decoration.
> Ernest Hemingway

There is nothing to writing. All you do is sit down at a typewriter and bleed.
> Ernest Hemingway

Close the door. Write with no one looking over your shoulder. Don't try to figure out what other people want to hear from you; figure out what you have to say. It's the one and only thing you have to offer.
> Barbara Kingsolver

Words are the most powerful drug used by mankind.

> Rudyard Kipling

There are three rules for writing. Unfortunately, no one can agree what they are.

> Somerset Maugham

I love writing. I love the swirl and swing of words as they tangle with human emotions.

> James A. Michener

Writing is its own reward.

> Henry Miller

We write to taste life twice, in the moment and in retrospect.

> Anaïs Nin

Words are a lens to focus one's mind.

> Ayn Rand

Writing is a way of talking without being interrupted.

> Jules Renard

Every writer is a narcissist. This does not mean that he is vain; it only means that he is hopelessly self-absorbed.
Leo Rosten

A blank piece of paper is God's way of telling us how hard it is to be God.
Sidney Sheldon

Most writers regard the truth as their most valuable possession, and therefore are most economical in its use.
Mark Twain

I'm writing a book. I've got the page numbers done.
Stephen Wright

Exercise the writing muscle every day, even if it is only a letter, notes, a title list, a character sketch, a journal entry. Writers are like dancers, like athletes. Without that exercise, the muscles seize up.
Jane Yolen

Writing is thinking on paper.
William Zinsser

Afterword

Hello, allow me to introduce myself.

Many years ago, with a B.A. in English and no idea what to do with it, I followed a dream and joined the U.S. Peace Corps. I worked as an English teacher and teacher trainer in Togo, West Africa. In the mean time, every university got computerized and when I went back to graduate school, I was bug-eyed while formatting my Master's thesis on a cute Apple MacIntosh computer. I've been in awe of computers ever since.

I never quite acclimated back into life in the United States or even a place that had snow in winter. So, I've been an expatriate for over 24 years, mostly in warm climes. But I do love to travel and visit my family, friends and Costco in the U.S. I was born in the great state of New Jersey, and today I live in Israel less than a mile from the Mediterranean Sea.

I'm not so secretly hooked on the internet and had to buy a separate computer for my work projects so that I can stay away from it. The city I live in is just right for me as I can dress as casually as I want every day without being the worst-dressed person in town and scoot around to all my errands on my bicycle as well as go to the beach whenever I want.

At the top of my gratitude lists are my eyes which enable me to indulge in reading every day. I have hundreds of books in my kindle library and on my computer, but I'm not ready to let go of all those paper books gathering dust. I'm proud to be part of the great generation that remembers what it was like to type on typewriters and can appreciate both books and "smart" devices.

Without naming all the names, hearty thanks are due to my husband, son, and special friends who've supported many a vision I've had as I've undergone a "mid-life crisis" of at least 10 years. Nowadays, my weekdays include teaching and participation in workshops and conferences along with various entrepreneurial putterings on the computer and occasionally cooking good food while singing Broadway show music.

Please, contact me to share your experiences and watch for my further writings. Let me know how you use your journal writing; share with me quotes you love, and let me know if I've botched any of the quotations or attributions in this book.

Every writer needs social support which can include reviews at Amazon.com. I greatly appreciate all words that are honestly sent to me personally or on the facebook group: New Vision Publications -Independent publishers.

Join me in spreading good feelings in the world. Share your copy of this book with your own inner circle. Better yet, start over after a year with your copy (now personalized and decorated?) and buy additional copies as presents for everyone you know so that you support my future projects.

Invite me to speak to your group or conference. I conduct one-time workshops and on-going courses in areas of well-being including:

Journal-writing for self-therapy
Cultivate Joy and well-being
Positive Psychology
Stress Reduction 101
Discover your inner teacher
Creative journaling

With love and joy,

Judy

Write to me at judy@judyshafarman.net

www.judyshafarman.net

43000624R00147

Made in the USA
San Bernardino, CA
13 December 2016